PSALM 104: 1-3 "... O LORD MY GOD, THOU
ART VERY GREAT ... WHO
MAKETH
THE CLOUDS HIS CHARIOT:
WHO
WALKETH UPON THE WINGS
OF THE
WIND ..."

BALLOONING:
A PICTORIAL GUIDE AND WORLD DIRECTORY

BALLOONING: A PICTORIAL GUIDE AND WORLD DIRECTORY

BY: W.E. THRASHER

Thrasher Balloons Inc.
P.O. Box 1111
Homestead, Florida 33030

To the Malonys and memories of a fun Amazon River Cruise!
Keep looking up Hebrews 13:8
"Captain Crunch"
W.E.T.

Library of Congress catalog card number: 77-89039

ISBN 0-9601514-0-0

Dedicated to my wife Laura, and daughters Cheryl, Lynn and Patricia who not only tolerate but share my ballooning adventures.

TABLE OF CONTENTS

SECTION TWO

DIRECTORY

PSALM 18:10 AND HE RODE UPON A CHERUB,
AND DID FLY: YEA, HE DID FLY
UPON THE WINGS OF THE WIND.

SECTION I

INTRODUCTION

With the ever increasing number of books rolling off the presses, one might question the need for yet another, especially on balloons as these contrivances have been around since 1783. But while others deal with the historical or romantic aspect of the subject, this publication is exactly what the title promises, a pictorial guide and world directory. Photograph after photograph takes you right up front to a balloon launch, lets you see it firsthand, just as though you were there. And of course the directory section lists pilots all around the globe should you care to take a ride or learn to fly. Each and every name and address has been carefully checked for accuracy by direct correspondence with the pilot. All known manufacturers of balloons have been contacted. Those who responded are listed in the appropriate section.

So come fly with me in my beautiful balloon. As you view the scenes, try to imagine yourself in a crack of dawn setting, dew on the ground, the beautiful morning sun just peeking up on the eastern horizon, and perhaps a rooster crowing in the distance. You have another sip of coffee, pass the empty cup to one of the ground-crew members, and with a deep-throated blast of the burners, the hush of morning is broken. In a few seconds the stillness returns as your pilot closes the blast valve. Much to your surprise you notice you are already several feet off the ground. With the unmistakable broad smile of every first-timer, you're up, up and away!

BASICS OF BALLOON FLYING

A modern hot air balloon is simple to fly. As with anything else, the more you practice, the more proficient you become. Basically, here's how you do it. First, select a grassy field or pasture. If the wind is blowing, it is preferable to be protected by some large trees. Hook up the propane fuel tanks and strap them into the gondola, then check to see that all connections are tight. Now the load-lifting shroud cables are attached to the gondola, which is then laid over on its side, and the envelope is stretched out downwind. To put in the original air, we use a small gasoline-driven fan. This is placed on the ground several feet back from the mouth. The blower is started and two people hold open the mouth allowing the envelope to fill. When it is about half full the pilot turns on the burner and starts heating the air which expands it. The envelope then rises until it is standing above the gondola which has been brought upright by the envelope. Now the pilot increases the heat to match the load until the balloon is bouyant, then with a small amount of additional heat you very gently lift off the ground and you are on your way. The inflation takes about five minutes. In flight the pilot increases or decreases the heat in the envelope, causing the balloon to rise or descend. There are two methods of flying: one is to use a small amount of heat equal to the amount you are losing, thus allowing the balloon to fly itself: the other is to put in short full blasts of heat with long periods of silence in between (the latter is the more popular method). When you are ready to land, the balloon is brought down to a low altitude and you fly along until you see a field or pasture in your flight path, then just as you come over the edge of the field allow the envelope to cool and drop down for a landing.

The old Chinese saying that one picture is worth a thousand words may be trite, but it is very true. On the following pages we have illustrated the step-by-step procedure of a balloon inflation and flight. Welcome aboard, and we hope you will enjoy the "flight".

Captain Crunch

TETHER FLIGHT

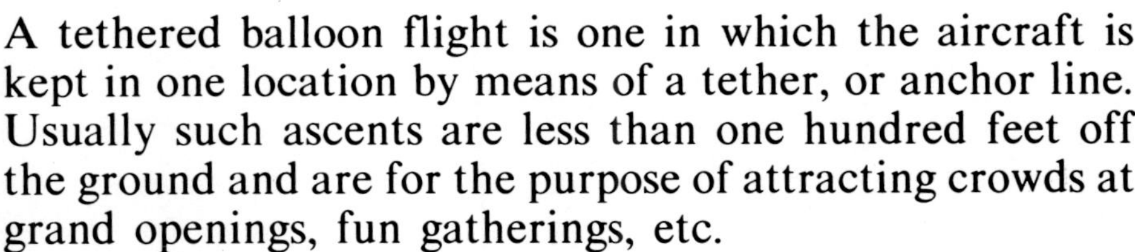

A tethered balloon flight is one in which the aircraft is kept in one location by means of a tether, or anchor line. Usually such ascents are less than one hundred feet off the ground and are for the purpose of attracting crowds at grand openings, fun gatherings, etc.

Photographs on pages 9 through 33 courtesy of Mr. Charles Rosendale and the Daily Courier, Connellsville, Pennsylvania.

Up at sunrise . . . unpacking.

Rolling out the envelope, still in a protective sleeve. Envelope weight is 124 pounds. (56 kilograms)

BRAVE
W

SEMCO
BALLOON

Instrument panel consisting of altimeter, vertical speed indicator, temperature gauge, and compass is strapped in place.

Since balloons share the same airspace as other aircraft including fully loaded commercial jetliners, it is understandable both the balloon and balloonist be licensed.

Either a Private or Commercial license may be earned. A comprehensive written exam, flight instruction dual and solo, and a flight check ride by an examiner are required prior to licensing.

Note the documents in full view, an F.A.A. requirement for all aircraft. A Standard Airworthiness Certificate, Certificate of Aircraft Registration (N-111LT), and a set of Operation Limitations must be carried on board at all times. Periodic inspections by authorized persons must be made, and appropriate entries placed in the aircraft log.

Mrs. Thrasher Sr. on left observes her first balloon launch with awe. The envelope covers an area more than 50 by 70 feet. (15 by 21 meters)

Daughter Cheryl and commercial pilot Laura prepare rip line which will later open top of balloon at end of flight.

Rings attached to each "gore" are alternately placed over the brass pin held by Laura. Gores are the tapering vertical pieces of fabric which make up the

balloon envelope. The number of gores varies from one manufacturer to another.

Wil holds rip line, the heavy braided steel cable in his right hand. This is fed through aluminum block held in left hand thus securing the brass pin.

Thread temporarily holds rip line in place during inflation. After the balloon is inflated, outward pressure takes over and a pull of more than 25 pounds (11 Kg) is required for deflation. A number of closure methods prevail in present day ballooning.

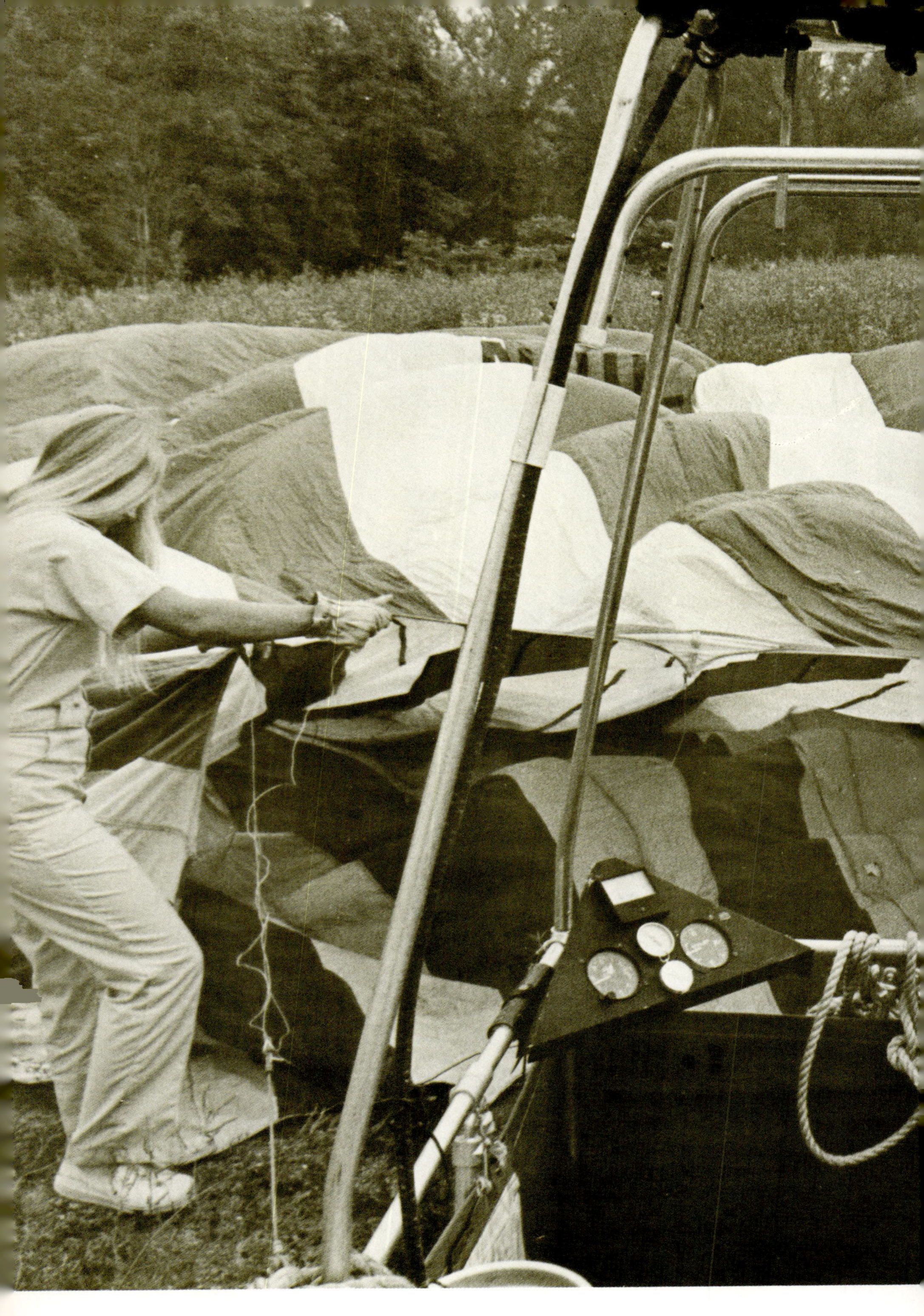

Ballooning is a team effort.

Gasoline-driven fan, out of camera range, is started and envelope billows.

A foot is placed on bottom of mouth at each side and the top is

lifted open to catch air from inflator. It fills in a matter of minutes.

INSIDE LOOKING OUT

Rip line and maneuvering vent line are laid aside. Hand held burner aids in even heating of air in envelope.

Main burners now on, Laura prepares to shut off hand held burner. Note the balloon is only partially inflated.

Recipe for FUN:

Take 2 pilots, 1 reporter, place under burner and simmer a couple hours until done. Serve with cold drinks in a picnic setting.

Fully inflated craft. Note the haze . . . frequently an indicator of calm winds. As morning fog "burns off" or dissipates, a great day for ballooning usually prevails.

An upward view from pilots position. Note maneuvering vent (patchlike square at lower left) which allows minor flight adjustments.

The captain thanks his crew.

Where there is a balloon, there is a camera!

FREE FLIGHT

A free flight is one in which the aircraft is not held in one location but rather travels with the wind. The pilot controls altitude, and as a result, his direction. Winds "at altitude" are frequently opposite "surface" winds, with an infinite number of combinations in between. This is just another reason why lighter-than-air flight is so challenging.

Photographs and story "Balloon To Balloon" courtesy of Mr. Wayne Green and 73 Magazine.

BALLOON TO BALLOON!

Early on the morning of May 18th, two giant balloons rose from the outskirts of Homestead, Florida, lifting two radio amateurs into the skies so that they could establish a new first . . . aerostat mobile amateur to aerostat mobile amateur two-way communication.

It all started a few weeks earlier when a letter from Wil Thrasher W4SAC (Captain Crunch) arrived at the 73 HQ in Peterborough suggesting the possibility of a new first for amateur radio . . . communications between balloons. Why not! I called Crunch and asked when I should be down for the event . . . cameras and courage in hand.

On the evening of the 17th Sherry Smythe and I headed for Miami, armed with cameras, lenses, HTs, and a CB rig for the rented car. The CB rig helped us to keep track of traffic on the hour drive to Homestead . . . and to find the motel when we got there.

We all assembled at Captain Crunch's home the next morning a little after 6:00 a.m. Present were Wil's wife Laura (EX-KN3DHI), the first licensed lady balloonist in Florida . . . Walt Farley K4QE . . . Ed Doll W4KLM (retired from A.T. & T.) . . . Captain Crunch (the second licensed balloonist in Florida) and John Mickel, a Florida smokey with a CB handle of Officer Friendly and a car license of FUZZ. John was taught ballooning by Wil and he, in turn taught Laura. John's chase car driver was Nancy Fortier, a Delta Airlines stewardess, who is working on her balloon license. Bill Otting, Wil's maintenance man, also helped get the balloons ready. The balloons were packed in very large hassock-type bags. Once out of the bag and stretched out on the grass they were amazingly big . . . about seventy feet long. It took three people to pull the protective sheath off the multicolored nylon material. The gondolas were quickly assembled, despite the multitudes of gnats, which were almost thick enough

Captain Crunch gets ready to unpack his balloon. It is a long thin sleeve for protection. At the left is the gondola, which breaks down in two parts for hauling around . . . the gasoline-powered fan for starting the balloon . . . and small propane tank for the hand-held burner. In the background, the second

balloon for the First Ham Radio Two Meter FM Two-Way Balloon Contact is being assembled. This is the balloon in which Wayne will go up, manned by John Mickel.

Ed Doll, W4KLM helps Wil Thrasher W4SAC (Captain Crunch) with the

balloon, while Bill Otting and Walt Farley K4QE remove the sleeve.

Laura Thrasher (ex KN3DHI), Florida's first licensed lady balloonist, fastens cables from balloon to gondola while Bill Otting and K4QE hold balloon.

Wayne (W2NSD) holds balloon envelope while Wil (W4SAC) removes the sleeve.

Balloon envelope is spread out and ready to be inflated.

A small gasoline-powered fan is used to start inflation of the balloon.

How the balloon looks from inside . . . W4SAC (Captain Crunch) on the right, K4QE on the left.

Once the envelope is inflated, the air has to be heated. Having served it's purpose, the ground inflator fan is shut off.

 As the air heats up, the balloon rises . . . here is John getting just the right amount of hot air into the balloon to keep it upright yet not have it take off before everyone is ready.

to drive off the mosquitoes ... but not quite. The two propane tanks were put into each gondola and strapped into place, with a pipe going to the burner located just below the open bottom of the envelope.

A gasoline powered fan was set up to blow air into the envelopes and they quickly billowed out ... with the help of my running around inside one pushing the material out to catch the air. Once the envelope was full of air from the fan, the propane burners were turned on and flames shot into the envelope. With this the balloon soon righted itself and had to be held down, while we waited for the second balloon to be inflated.

Soon we were ready to go. I stopped taking pictures of the preparations, gave one HT to Sherry for Wil to use ... she was going up with him ... gave one to W4KLM to coordinate the ground support (they had to follow us as we floated along so they could bring the balloon back after it had landed). Sherry also had a camera. John had his balloon about ready to take off so I hopped aboard, camera in one hand, lenses in my pockets, HT in the other hand, and trying to hold onto the gondola with an elbow as John turned on the propane. The air in the balloon has to be about 100° hotter than outside to get enough lift. It's a little scary with the flames shooting five or six feet up into the nylon balloon, roaring so you can't talk.

We lifted off at 7:22 a.m., just as smooth as you could ask. John said not to worry about the trees we were dragging through ... so I didn't ... it was just the top of the branches anyway. Soon we were several hundred feet up, with Crunch's balloon just a short way behind us. We'd go up and up ... then start to settle back down again. As we came down John would give a blast of the propane and we'd slow down ... then go back up again ... bobbing across the landscape.

The W4SAC balloon with Captain Crunch at the controls . . . Sherry Smythe boarding the gondola.

Here's the W4SAC (Captain Crunch) home. His balloon is about to take off for the historic ham QSO. (photo taken from the airborne balloon)

We are both airborne and the contact is made . . . W4SAC aerostat mobile four with W2NSD aerostat mobile four . . . like they say in the old movies . . . roger, over and out.

The two balloons make their way across southern Florida. Will they be blown out to sea and never heard from again? No . . . Wayne is busy making contacts via local repeaters with his ham rig. Wil is looking for a place to land . . . for coffee perhaps?

Not exactly Miami International Airport ... just an okra field a few miles from takeoff. By using just enough flames to keep the hot air right, it is possible to come down very gently.

We soon had out two-way amateur radio contact in the bag . . . 146.52 MHz FM . . . and two way with the ground to boot. Once that was done, I switched to some of the nearby repeaters and made a few contacts via them as a bonus.

On one of the descents we came down toward a field where a bunch of women were picking okra. We yelled "hello" to them and arranged to come down close enough so that they could throw an okra up to us. It was a fairly open field with a road leading into it so Crunch decided to end his flight there. He touched down gently and that was that. John and I went on a few miles further, with Nancy following in the FUZZ car. We eventually spotted a nice clear field ahead and plopped quietly into the middle of an exercise ring for horses.

Once down you have to collapse the envelope as quickly as you can so it won't be caught in a sudden breeze and drag you. We took our time . . . gave the balloon a little blast to make it lighter and walked it a couple hundred feet over to the road to deflate it there. You pull a ring and which opens up the whole top of the balloon, letting the hot air out.

Here's Wil with his trailer . . . it carries the balloon, gondola, and equipment for return home. For longer flights, or distant promotions his specially equipped Winnebago motor home is used.

Back at Crunch's home we played a tape of the morning's events and ate doughnuts. Laura has a fantastic organ setup and she played some music for us . . . in all, it was a most successful day.

Balloons are fun . . . no question about that at all. They run from about $5,000 on up, and can stay in the air three to four hours on two propane tanks. The balloon has a diameter of approximately fifty feet and goes up some seventy feet. It has a ceiling of about 20,000 feet . . . but this is higher than you want to go without oxygen.

While you don't have a lot of control over which direction you are going you can pick an elevation which has the winds you want. We were able to slow down and wait for Captain Crunch and Sherry to catch up with us by staying low and waiting for the higher winds to bring them up to us.

I sure want to thank Wil for setting up the event. He even brought in a second balloon from Atlanta for it. And I want to thank Laura, Walt, Ed, Nancy and Bill for helping out. Both Sherry and I had a wonderful time. Sherry had the same problems I did . . . she had binoculars around her neck, an HT in one hand, a camera in the other . . . and then she was told to hold on to the gondola!

What with trying to keep in touch with Captain Crunch in the other balloon, Ed on the ground, hold onto the gondola, and take pictures with various long lenses, I had my hands and pockets full. When you're up in the air about 500 feet you have a sort of automatic need to hold onto something. Tight!

COMMERCIAL APPLICATIONS

The primary commercial use of balloons is in advertising. Whether it be a grand opening, political rally, or Sunday school project, balloons do capture attention. Balloons frequently appear in television commercials and have also been used for such diverse activities as logging in the Pacific Northwest and various military exercises.

The Porter Paints balloon piloted by James H. Davis shows a typical logo display on the envelope. This balloon is an AX-9 category of 140,000 cubic feet capacity. (3920 cubic meters) It is type certified for eight occupants, and is the largest hot air balloon regularly taken on free flights in the United States of America. The aircraft has been to 38,300 feet (11,673 meters) on an altitude record attempt and is pictured here with a small basket used for that venture.

Photo courtesy Porter Paint Co.
Louisville, Kentucky

Porter
Paints

Cathay Pacific Airways balloons over the New Territories of Hong Kong.

Photo Courtesy
Captain G. Green
Cathay Pacific Airways
Kai Tak Airport
Hong Kong

This balloon recently trailed a leg of bacon across Loch Ness in a vain attempt to catch the legendary monster.

Commercial pilot Laura Thrasher, Florida's first lady balloonist at the controls. Photos such as this one make interesting handout literature at promotional events. The reverse may carry technical information on the aircraft as well as a sponsors message.

Author Wil Thrasher left, and daughter Patty with Homestead News Leader editor Paul Brookshire. (Note gondola advertising)

Photo by Phillip Blaha

A "SPOOF" TICKET AND MORE FREE NEWSPAPER PUBLICITY

Photo by Laura Thrasher

This four hour unannounced tether flight resulted in: (1) Sun Line Cruises advertising (2) Redland Racquet Club advertising (3) youth choir light bulbs sold (4) one new student for balloon instruction, not to mention the long term exposure in this book for those who sponsored the flight.

Photo by Laura Thrasher

Homestead Newspaper editor Paul Brookshire operating the blast valve while Cheryl and Lynn Thrasher display ad for Princeton Nazarene Church Choir project. (Photo by Phillip Blaha)

"Sounds Great" flown by David Claridge in England. Balloon is an orange and purple Thunder.

Joseph Starkbaum of Austria promoting British Petroleum

The familiar Ford logo on a balloon in Denmark

Photo courtesy Danish Balloon Club

Phillipians 2:9 "... GOD RAISED HIM UP TO THE HEIGHTS OF HEAVEN AND GAVE HIM A NAME WHICH IS ABOVE EVERY OTHER NAME ..."

SECTION II
Directory

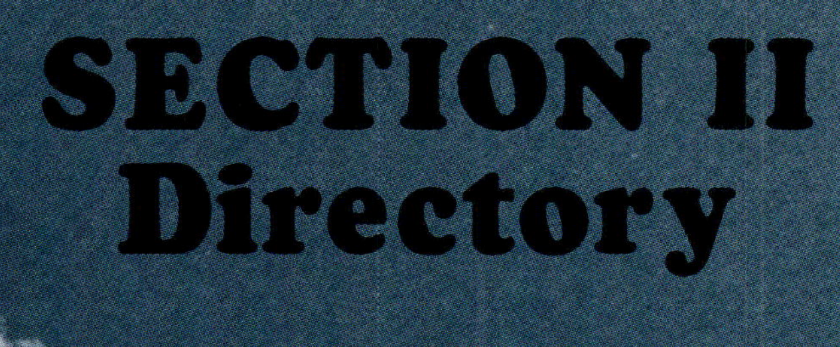

Neither the author nor the publisher assumes responsibility for errors or omissions. Corrections or additions may be submitted to W.E. Thrasher, P.O. Box 1111 Homestead, Florida 33030 for inclusion in future editions of this directory.

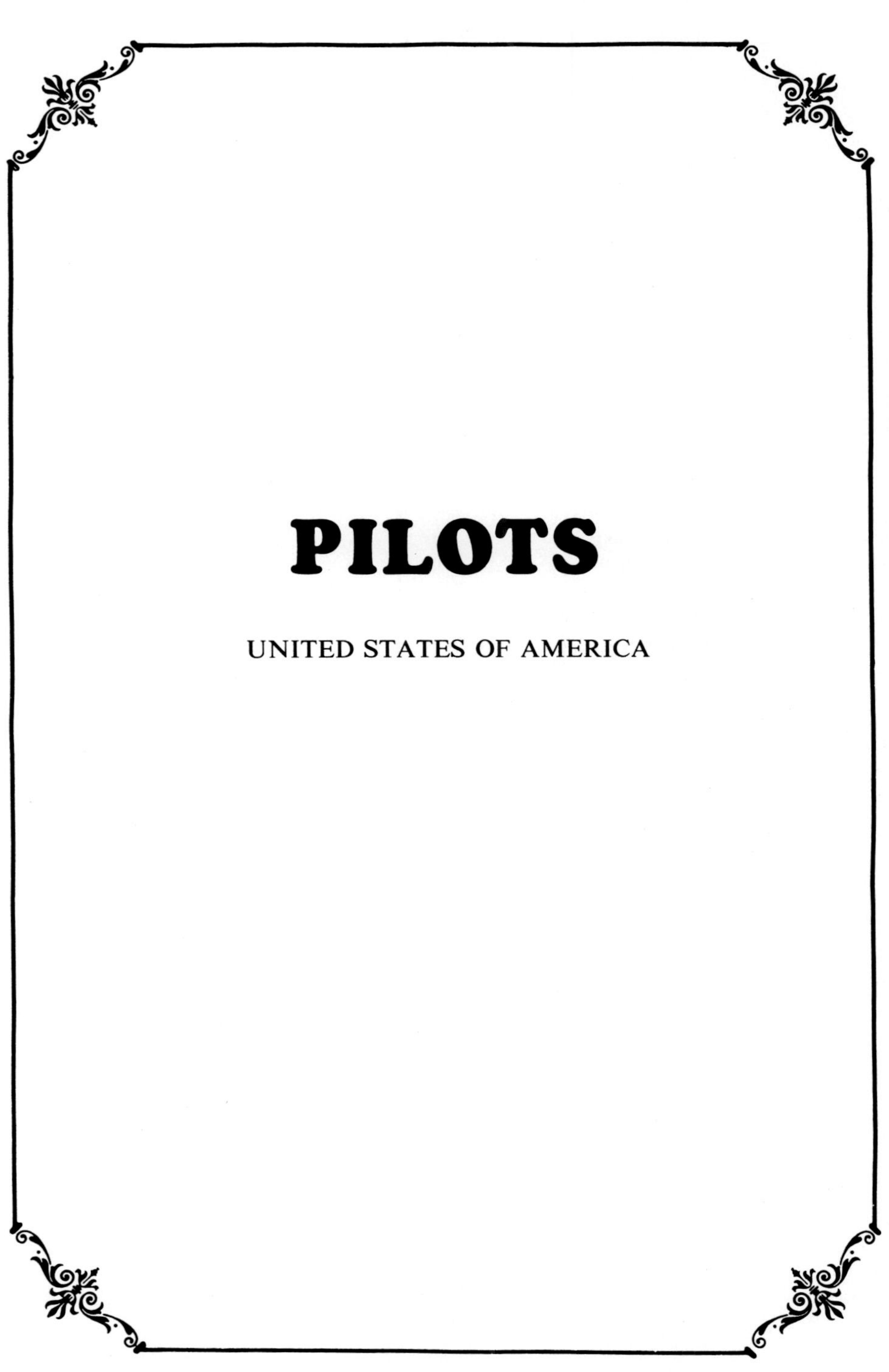

PILOTS

UNITED STATES OF AMERICA

ARIZONA

CORY, DOUGLAS W.
210 W. BENTON AVE.
FLAGSTAFF, AZ 86001

GORRELL, FRED T.
501 E. PORT AU PRINCE LN.
PHOENIX, AZ 85022

GREEN, THOMAS J.
4620 VIA ENTRADA
TUCSON, AZ 85718

HOOVER, CHARLES R.
2932 N. MANOR DR. — WEST
PHOENIX, AZ 85014

JEWETT, WILLIAM R.
3095 AVENUE -A-
YUMA, AZ 85364

KASPRZYK, JR., STAN J.
P.O. BOX 1112
WILLIAMS AFB, AZ 85224

KENNELLY, LYNN
6841A EAST OSBORN
SCOTTSDALE, AZ 85252

KITCHEL, JAMES D.
C-O CAT BALLOON, INC.
2911 E. SHERRAN LANE
PHOENIX, AZ 85016

MILLER, GEORGIA
2210 N. 9th Ave.
PHOENIX, AZ 85012

MILLER, WILLIAM E.
2210 N. 9th AVE.
PHOENIX, AZ 85012

PITRAT, CLAUDE H.
RTE 1 — BOX 61
LAVEEN, AZ 85339

RUST, EVANS M.
2816 N. SCOTTSDALE RD #1
SCOTTSDALE, AZ 85257

SMITH, DOUG
16026 N. 23RD AVE.
PHOENIX, AZ 85023

THRUMAN, JANET
8226 E. VALLEYVIEW RD.
SCOTTSDALE, AZ 85253

WATSON, RICHARD J.
7616 N. 12TH ST. #129
PHOENIX, AZ 85020

ARKANSAS

CREECH, JAMES E.
139½ SOUTHWEST DR.
JONESBORO, AR 72401

HEARIN, DON E.
2210 JUNCTION RD.
EL DORADO, AR 71730

LANGFORD, ROBERT M.
RTE 6 — BOX 361
JONESBORO, AR 72401

MUNDAY, BILL
2001 RESERVOIR #8
LITTLE ROCK, AR 72207

WEAR, PHILLIP C.
6420 SO. -Q- ST.
FT. SMITH, AR 72903

Ted Farrell's "Teddy Bear"
Rolling Hills, California

CALIFORNIA

BARTLETT, PHIL
c/o HOTEL EUREKA
195 PICKERING AVE.
FREMONT, CA 94536

BARTLETT, SHIRLEY W.
P.O. BOX 2652
NILES, CA 94536

BENNETT, GORDON L.
415 ALLEN STREET
ARROYO GRANDE, CA 93420

BECK, ROBERT L.
221 EDGEMONT DR.
REDLANDS, CA 92373

BENNETT, GORDON L.
415 ALLEN STREET
ARROYO GRANDE, CA 93420

BURMEISTER, NAT S.
3145 ROCKLIN DR.
SANTA ROSA, CA 95405

CALLICRATE, PAUL V.
305 VALLEJO ST.
PETALUMA, CA 94952

CAVANAUGH, ALFRED G.
185 RISHELL DR.
OAKLAND, CA 94619

CERVENY, EUGENE P.
127 CONCORD ST.
GLENDALE, CA 91203

CHAMBERS, J. REBER
572 S. SWIDLER PL.
ORANGE, CA 92669

CLIFFORD, RONALD E.
2476 BALFOUR CT.
NAPA, CA 94558

COLLINS, M. RAYMOND
505 CASHEW CT.
SAN RAMON, CA 94583

CRISWELL, C.L. (TEX)
10623 LARCH AVE.
BLOOMINGTON, CA 92316

DAVIS, DON A.
39 NIETO AVE.
LONG BEACH, CA 90803

DUFF, RODERIC B.
BOX 3682
GLENDALE, CA 91201

ECKFORD, JIM F.
111 YALE RD.
MENLO PARK, CA 94205

FARNHAM, CAPT. MICK
FARNHAM ENTERPRISES
1033 CRANBERRY DR.
CUPERTINO, CA 95014

FARRELL, TED
4 RINGBIT RD. WEST
ROLLING HILLS, CA 90274

FETTERLY, JEANINE
1793 NORTHWOOD CT.
OAKLAND, CA 94611

FETTERLY, LARRY L.
1793 NORTHWOOD CT.
OAKLAND, CA 94611

CALIFORNIA

FINGERG, STANLEY C.
19475 MONTEVINA RD.
LOS GATOS, CA 95030

GROVE, RONALD G.
133 VISTA DE LA CUMBRE
SANTA BARBARA, CA 93105

HALL, GORDON L.
3801 MEADOWLANE AVE.
BAKERSFIELD, CA 93309

HAYES, DR. WILL
400 VIA DICHOSA
HOPE RANCH
SANTA BARBARA, CA 93110

HOLZ, CARL E.
2055 MARSH RD.
SANTA ROSA, CA 95401

KENDRICK, EUGENE A.
2033 S. WHITE RD.
SAN JOSE, CA 95122

KRIEG, FRED W.
246 LOMITA DR. — BOX 1147
PERRIS, CA 92370

LANCE, JACK R.
5820 FAIR OAKS BLVD.
CARMICHAEL, CA 95608

LOCKHEED BALLOON CLUB
c/o LERA BLDG. #160
P.O. BOX 504
SUNNYVALE, CA 94086

MULLIN, CHRISTOPHER E.
P.O. BOX 121
TIBURON, CA 94920

MUNDAY, DICK
TRUCKEE BALLOON WORKS
BOX 2456
OLYMPIC VALLEY, CA 95730

NEUSHUL, PETER C.
NEUSHUL CORPORATION
1911 W. 139TH ST.
GARDENA, CA 90249

PATTON, ROBERT L.
507 HARVARD RD. APT. C
BURBANK, CA 91501

PEABODY, LAURENCE
952 W. 17TH STREET, APT. A
COSTA MESA, CA 92627

PEARLMAN, EDWIN C.
2274 RIORDAN DR.
SAN JOSE, CA 95130

PICCARD, DON
P.O. BOX 1902
NEWPORT BEACH, CA 92663

PINGREY, RICHARD H.
114 SANDALWOOD CT.
SANTA ROSA, CA 95401

RECHS, ROBERT J.
8157 MADISON AVE.
SOUTH GATE, CA 90280

ROBILLARD, CHRISTOPHER
17 SUNDANCE DR.
NEWPORT BEACH, CA 92663

ROSS, JAMES T.
12706 BLACKTHORN ST.
GARDEN GROVE, CA. 92640

Imagine dropping by your neighborhood hamburger stand in one of these!

CALIFORNIA

SANDEEN, GARNET G. PhD.
2718 SANDPIPER DR.
COSTA MESA, CA 92626

SAPP, JONATHAN W.
1600 DONNER AVE.
SAN FRANCISCO, CA 94124

SCHLOSSBERG, JR., BEN
2249 LINNINGTON AVE.
LOS ANGELES, CA 92037

SIMMONDS, JONATHAN R.
LT — U.S.N.
VXE — 6
N.S. POINT MUGU, CA 93041

SONNICHSEN, DEKE
BALLOONS AND AIRSHIPS — WEST
BOX 2247
MENLO PARK, CA 94025

STOCKWELL, BRENT
BALLOON EXCELSIOR, INC.
1241 HIGH ST.
OAKLAND, CA 94601

THORNTON, RONALD D.
20975 VALLEY GREEN DR. 243
CUPERTINO, CA 95014

TOBY, GILBERT W.
429 PINE ST. APT. A
MONTEREY, CA 93940

VALE, JAY M.
20852 ELENDA DR.
CUPERTINO, CA 95014

WALLIS, JOHN ANTHONY
54 UTAH AVE.
WOODLAND, CA 95695

WILSON, DONALD R.
816 COLUSA
BERKELEY, CA 94707

COLORADO

BARZ, JR., DON H.
8393 W. QUAY DR.
ARVADA, CO 80003

BARZ, PATRICIA L.
8393 W. QUAY DR.
ARVADA, CO 80003

BELL, FREDERICK F.
1225 S. GAYLORD
DENVER, CO 80210

BELL, FREDERICK W.
1225 S. GAYLORD
DENVER, CO 80210

BELL, LOIS C.
1225 S. GAYLORD
DENVER, CO 80210

BERGER, MIKE
15306 E. PENWOOD PL.
DENVER, CO 80232

BUNDGAARD, ROBERT M.
2424 S. YOURK #202
DENVER, CO 80210

CARTER, JR., JAMES D.
46 MAC ARTHUR
PUEBLO, CO 81001

CORDER, L. KEVAN
15793 DE GAULLE CIRCLE
BOX 241
BRIGHTON, CO 80601

COLORADO

DAVIES, THOMAS A.
14 BROOKSIDE DR.
LITTLETON, CO 80121

EOFF, CAROLYN S.
7429 W. 74TH AVE.
ARVADA, CO 80003

IDA, DONALD H.
6892 S. PRINCE CIRCLE
LITTLETON, CO 80120

KENNY, ROBERT L.
1506 S. TERRY
LONGMONT, CO 80501

LIFE CYCLE BALLOON SCHOOL
1224 15TH LARIMER SQUARE
DENVER, CO 80202

MAGGARD, ETSLE D.
509 FIRESIDE ST.
LOUISVILLE, CO 80027

PARK, DENNIS P.
P.O. BOX 3424
USAF ACADEMY, CO 80541

PFISTER, BETTY
P.O. BOX EE
ASPEN, CO 81611

RIDER, FRANK E.
STAR ROUTE BOX 41
DEL NORTE, CO 81132

ROY, DON L.
P.O. BOX 5834
USAF ACADEMY, CO 80841

SCHEER, KENNETH E.
5206 ALLISON ST.
ARVADA, CO 80002

SIBILA, DAVID V.
20172 CYPRESS DR.
MORRISON, CO 80465

TEPPER, JERRY J.
7201 N. SHERIDAN
ARVADA, CO 80002

TONGISH, MARION J.
10 CHEERYMOORE DRIVE
ENGLEWOOD, CO 80110

VANDE HOEF, JOYCE E.
2424 SO. YORK #202
DENVER, CO. 80210

WELLENS, BRUCE M.
2001 ELIZABETH
PUEBLO, CO 81003

WIANT, TRACI
EDWARDS HALL RM 366
FT. COLLINS, CO 80521

CONNECTICUT

BATCHELLER, ROBERT A.
22 VILLAGE ST.
E. HARTFORD, CT 06108

BOLAND, BRIAN J.
PINE DR. RD 2
BURLINGTON, CT 06013

FOSTER, GILBERT R.
RTE 2 BOX 190
STONINGTON, CT 06378

Johnny Jennings of Greenwood Mississippi and balloon "Miss Cotton". Background setting is old colonial home in Atalla County and the "Ole South" Labor Day festivities, September 1977.

CONNECTICUT

HAVILL, REGINALD W.
6 WOODCHUCK LANE
WILTON, CT 06897

ISLER, JIM
15 N. QUAKER LANE
W. HARTFORD, CT 06119

JOHNSON, STEPHEN C.
249 WEST LANE
RIDGEFIELD, CT 06877

JOHNSTON, RICHARD W.
BRICK HOUSE — GRISWOLD PT.
OLD LYME, CT 06371

MELLICK, ORVILLE W.
22 ALDEN RD.
GREENWICH, CT 06830

MINO, WILLIAM H.
60 WILLIAMS STREET
GLASTONBURY, CT 06033

STUMPF, PAUL S.
28 LEDGEWOOD DR.
FARMINGTON, CT 06032

DISTRICT OF COLUMBIA

PARKINSON, RUSSELL J.
724 — 7TH ST SE APT 2
WASHINGTON, DC 20003

FLORIDA

ALLEN, JAMES E.
401 CRESCENT DR.
MIAMI SPRINGS, FL 33166

ANDERSON, GREGORY D.
2630 HIBISCUS ST.
SARASOTA, FL 33580

BALLOON WORLD
476 MAGNOLIA ST.
ORMOND BCH., FL 32074

BOWCOCK, JR., HAROLD M.
11325 SIXTH ST. EAST
TREASURE IS., FL 33706

BROWN, JR., RAYMOND J.
5423 GLORIANNE CIRCLE N.
JACKSONVILLE, FL 32207

CENTRAL FLA CLOUD CLIMBERS
BALLOON CLUB
966B E. MICHIGAN AVE.
ORLANDO, FL 32806

CHARLES, WILLIAM W.
2265 MIDDLETON AVE.
WINTER PARK, FL 32792

CLEGG, FREDERICK LEE
11345 — 6TH ST. EAST
TREASURE IS, FL 33706

EDGETT, B. DAVID
RTE 3 — BOX 327
MIDDLEBURG, FL 32068

ELGIE, DALE E.
9300 SW 104TH ST.
MIAMI, FL 33156

FLORIDA

GOLDEN, GLENN W.
1412 SAN JOSE BLVD.
HOLLY HILL, FL 32017

HARNDEN, CRAIG
7400 SW 68 CT.
S. MIAMI, FL 33143

HICKEY, JOHN B.
2506 PARKLAND BLVD.
TAMPA, FL. 33609

JOHNSON, WAYNE
13825 SW 79 CT.
MIAMI, FL 33158

LA MERE, EDDIE D.
306 W. SLIGH
TAMPA, FL 33604

LYONS, HAL
1215 — 15TH AVE. NORTH
ST. PETERSBURG, FL 33702

MILLER, DICK
7215 SW 105 TER.
MIAMI, FL 33156

MORAN, JOHN
7945 CAMINO CIRCLE
MIAMI, FL 33143

PAGE, BRIAN
22319 SW 103 AVE.
BOX 4,
MIAMI, FL 33190

REESOR, THOMAS W.
332 PLANT AVE.
TAMPA, FL 33606

RIVERS, TIM
306 W. SLIGH
TAMPA, FL 33604

ROBERTS, JR., STEVE W.
420 W. MAIN ST.
AVON PARK, FL 33825

ROHR, CHUCK
1407 E. LAS OLAS
FT. LAUDERDALE, FL 33301

ROMERO, NELSON
7030B W. HILLSBOROUGH AVE.,
TAMPA, FL 33614

SETTECASI, JOSEPH C.
707 ALFRED ST.
TAMPA, FL 33603

SMITH, CHARLES A., JR.
9362 SW 35TH ST.
MIAMI, FL 33165

SPOHRER, B.F.
2901 S. BAYSHORE DR. 15C
MIAMI, FL 33133

SPROTT, JR., KINGSWOOD
P.O. BOX 2718
LAKELAND, FL 33803

THRASHER, LAURA B.
P.O. BOX 1111
HOMESTEAD, FL 33030

THRASHER, WILBERT E.
P.O. BOX 1111
HOMESTEAD, FL 33030

FLORIDA

URIBE, MIGUEL
1111 CRANDON BLVD. C1006
KEY BISCAYNE, FL 33149

GEORGIA

ADAMS, MIKE
c/o MIKE ADAMS BALLOON LOFT
P.O. BOX 12168
ATLANTA, GA. 30355

GORE, EDWARD
2484 BURTON CIRCLE
MORROW, GA 30260

HEAD, TARP
c/o MIKE ADAMS BALLOON LOFT
P.O. BOX 12168
ATLANTA, GA 30355

HUDGENS, HAROLD R., JR.
1806 MARBURY LANE
ALBANY, GA 31707

MICKEL, JOHN T.
RTE 2 STANLEY ROAD
FAYETTEVILLE, GA 30214

MURPHY, TOBY
c/o MIKE ADAMS BALLOON LOFT
P.O. BOX 12168
ATLANTA, GA 30355

QUIRE, BRENDA G.
20 28TH ST. N.W.
ATLANTA, GA. 30309

SEMICH, BETTY
RTE 3, BOX 514 AERODROME WAY
GRIFFIN, GA 30223

SEMICH, MARK
SEMCO BALLOON
RTE 3 BOX 514 AERODROME WAY
GRIFFIN, GA 30223

SHIREY, WAYNE
261 CROGAN ST.
LAWRENCEVILLE, GA 30245

WILEY, JOE
213 ALLEN ST.
SUMMERVILLE, GA 30747

IDAHO

BUROKER, GLADYS E.
ROUTE 1 — BOX 98B
ATHOL, ID 83801

IDAHO BALLOON ADVENTURES
SPENCER, SCOTT LESLIE
106 ROGER STREET
BOISE, ID 83705

ILLINOIS

ALBERT, TERRY C.
21730 BOSCHOME RD. WEST
KILDEER, IL 60047

ASHLEIGH-MORGAN, CLAUDIA T.
285 DONLEA ROAD
BARRINGTON HILLS, IL 60010

ILLINOIS

BASS, JR., L. ARVIL
537 N. PLUM
HAVANA, IL 62644

BIRGE, KENNETH W.
58 HANOVER CT.
CHAMPAIGN, IL 61820

BONNER, JOHN M.
RTE 4
PARIS, IL 61944

BRUMM, STEVEN H.
506 S. DIVISION ST.
MAHOMET, IL 61853

COHEN, JR., M.S.
P.O. BOX 685
BARRINGTON, IL 60010

ESCH, ROBERT W.
415 W. UNION ST.
EDWARDSVILLE, IL 62025

FALK, PATRICIA A.
3246 W. WELLINGTON
CHICAGO, IL 60618

GARROTT, JERRY L.
9052 N. LOCUST LANE
PEORIA, IL 61614

HAYES, CHARLES M.
306 JACKSON ST.
PARK FOREST, IL 60466

HEURLIN, JR., USAF COL. VIC
305 S. ALBERT ST.
MT. PROSPECT, IL 60056

HIPPLER, STEVEN J.
201 W. MAIN ST.
CARY, IL 60013

JOHNSON, RAYMOND J.
817 S. FOURTH ST.
LIBERTYVILLE, IL 60048

JONES, PAUL A.
BOX 143
BUCKINGHAM, IL 60917

NEULANDER, STEPHEN
1047 WILMOT
DEERFIELD, IL 60015

O CONNELL, THOMAS J.
8506 W. 122ND PLACE
PALOS PARK, IL 60464

PITCHER, MERRITT W.
RTE 2
MORRISON, IL 61270

PLATT, CHARLES A.
P.O. BOX 1774
DECATUR, IL 62525

POORE, JOHN R.W.
BOX 29
HAMBURG, IL 62045

REAM, JOSEPH B.
FLYING TOMATO INC.
707 S. WRIGHT ST.
CHAMPAIGN, IL 61820

ROTHERT, EUGENE A.
201 HILLCREST DR.
ALGONQUIN, IL 60102

Laura Thrasher demonstrates tether flight for the camera.

ILLINOIS

SENN, A. RALPH
707 S. WRIGHT
CHAMPAIGN, IL 61820

SPITZ, ROBERT W.
2868 WESTERN AVE.
PARK FOREST, IL 60466

STELLAS, DEAN
1729 GROVE ST.
GLENVIEW, IL 60025

STEPHAN, GERALD F.
BOX 285
ALGONQUIN, IL 60102

STROUSE, JR., HARRY D.
352 ARROWHEAD LANE
BARRINGTON, IL 60010

VAN VALKENBURGH, JAMES J.
4157 MADISON AVE.
BROOKFIELD, IL 60513

WUJEK, FRED H.
1216 NINTH ST.
LA SALLE, IL 61301

INDIANA

BOBEL, DAVID R.
259 N. DUKES
PERU, IN 46970

BROWN, ROBERT F.
P.O. BOX 51
CORYDON, IN 47112

COFFIN, JOHN M.
3407 LORAL DR.
ANDERSON, IN 46013

DONNELLY, RICHARD L.
1111 IRVING WAY
ANDERSON, IN. 46011

LA GRAND, WILLIAM L.
823 WEBSTER
FT. WAYNE, IN 46802

MENCHHOFER, DONALD L.
6350 JOHNSON RD.
INDIANAPOLIS, IN 46220

MENCHHOFER, JEFF
6350 JOHNSON RD.
INDIANAPOLIS, IN 46220

OLIVER, WILLIAM
2803 BROWNCLIFF
BLOOMINGTON, IN 47401

SANKOWSKI, JOHN T.
3410 FRANKLIN ST.
HIGHLAND, IN 46322

SISSON, FRED P.
BOX 218
NASHVILLE, IN 47448

TARTER, GARY L.
10226 SHALLOW BROOK CT.
INDIANAPOLIS, IN 46229

THIEL, DAVID R.
3505 W. 61ST ST.
INDIANAPOLIS, IN 46208

IOWA

ALLEN, DEE ANN
413 NO. -K- ST.
INDIANOLA, IA 50125

IOWA

ALLSUP, SHERRY C.
412 NO. -K- ST.
INDIANOLA, IA 50125

BABER, DR. WILLIAM E.
1319 N. 13TH ST.
FT. DODGE, IA 50501

BARTHOLOMEW, JR., ROBERT
RR 2
CARLISLE, IA 50047

BEUKELMAN, DAVID P.
1508 ELEVENTH AVE. N.
FT. DODGE, IA 50501

CADWELL, JAMES L.
1004 — 10TH AVE. EAST
OSKALOOSA, IA 52577

CATTELL, DENNIS R.
2039 NW HICKORY LANE
ANKENY, IA 50021

DAVISON, DENNIS M.
1312 GREENFIELD
MARSHALLTOWN, IA 50158

DINKLER, EARL T.
47-B SCHILLETTER
AMES, IA 50012

DOCKSTADER, NORMAN L.
7200 NW 21ST
ANKENY, IA 50021

DRAKE, RICHARD R.
RADCLIFFE, IA 50230

FREEMAN, THOMAS E.
436 — 4TH
W. DES MOINES, IA 50265

GARVIN, STEVEN C.
505 E. MISSISSIPPI DR.
MUSCATINE, IA 52761

GOBLE, KENT P.
9275 GOLDEN VALLEY DR.
NORWALK, IA 50211

GRANT, CHARLES J.
1236 NO. 23RD ST.
FT. DODGE, IA 50501

GUENTHER, JEROME H.
4795 TRAILS END RD.
BETTENDORF, IA 52722

HUMES, JAMES T.
1317 — 10TH AVE. NORTH
FT. DODGE, IA 50501

JOHNSON, JOHN JOSEPH
428 — 28TH SW
MASON CITY, IA 50401

KURTZ, RONALD J.
2220 CHESTNUT CT. NE
CEDAR RAPIDS, IA 52402

LAWSON, BLAIR W.
1506 WEST 6TH
INDIANOLA, IA 50125

LINDEBERG, STEPHEN C.
P.O. BOX 1237
FT. DODGE, IA 50501

The Champion 'Special Shape' hot air balloon is a 1:500 scale flying model of the standard 3 inch 14mm Champion Spark Plug, and is the most technically intricate hot air balloon shape in the world. Courtesy Cameron Balloons.

IOWA

MARK, DANIEL LEE
835 E. EUCLID
DES MOINES, IA 50316

MART, TED L.
R.R. 4
KNOXVILLE, IA 50138

MC CRARY, RICHARD D.
7208 WASHINGTON
DES MOINES, IA 50311

MC GINLEY, WILLIAM F.
2108 N. LINWOOD AVE.
DAVENPORT, IA 52804

MORRIS, DAVID L.
FREDERICKSBURG, IA 50630

OERMAN, THOMAS
113 PARK ST.
MUSCATINE, IA 52761

RILEY, JERRY T.
205 E. KENTUCKY
INDIANOLA, IA 50125

ROSENDAHL, FRITZ
BOX 111
OKOBOJI, IA 51355

RUBLE, GARY
1201 NORTH -C-
INDIANOLA, IA 50125

SARGENT, MARY LOU
702 W. DETROIT APT. 2
INDIANOLA, IA 50125

SARGENT, THOMAS E.
702 W. DETROIT, APT. 2
INDIANOLA, IA 50125

SMEDAL, ZOE N.
1207 -H- AVE.
NEVADA, IA 50201

TALLANT, DAVID E.
4211 SW 5TH
DES MOINES, IA 50315

TINKER III, LEONARD E.
9275 GOLDEN VALLEY DR.
NORWALK, IA 50211

WUNDER, GAIGE L.
RTE 2
POSTVILLE, IA 52162

KANSAS

BLODGETT, HOLLY J.
1926 NE 35TH
TOPEKA, KS 66617

BROWN, MARION EUGENE
4921 N.E. KINCAID ROAD
TOPEKA, KS 66617

BRUSO, DR., JAMES H.
315 HIGHLAND DR.
PARSONS, KS 67357

CLARK, DENNIS T.
905 SECOND
GARDEN CITY, KS 67846

GIMBLET, KENNETH L.
P.O. BOX 765
LAWRENCE, KS 66044

KANSAS

HALL, J. GARTH
9734 BIRCH
WICHITA, KS 67212

HEBRLEE, BUD
P.O. BOX 1171
GARDEN CITY, KS 67846

HOOVER, FRANK W.
THE WALKWAY LEVEL
4TH FINANCIAL CT.
WICHITA, KS 67202

HYDE, CARLA D.
5020 W. 67TH ST.
SHAWNEE MISSION, KS 66208

HYDE, "FRED" L.L.
5020 W. 67TH ST.
SHAWNEE MISSION, KS 66208

HYDE, MARK L.
5020 W. 67TH ST.
SHAWNEE MISSION, KS 66208

MARTIN, ANTHONY W.
1120 HARDING
GARDEN CITY, KS 67846

ROBISON, ROLAND E.
RTE #4
PARSONS, KS 67357

ROESCH, ROBERT D.
1318 COOLIDGE
WICHITA, KS 67203

SIEFKES, JOHN E.
7 SWALLOW
WICHITA, KS 67230

SPURRIER, SANDRA A.
1702 NO. PINECREST
WICHITA, KS 67208

TANTILLO, CHARLES R.
3861 CHELMSFORD
TOPEKA, KS 66602

TOWSEND, BOB E.
1606 N. 3RD ST.
GARDEN CITY, KS 67846

WILCOX, CAROLE N.
ROUTE 2
ANTHONY, KS 67003

WILCOX, HERBERT L.
RTE 2
ANTHONY, KS 67003

KENTUCKY

BLANKENSHIP, JOHN R., JR.
100 E HEBRON LN — BOX 256A
SHEPHERDSVILLE, KY 40165

COHEN, NORMAN K.
SUITE 3372
1169 EASTERN PARKWAY
LOUISVILLE, KY 40222

DAVIS, DANIEL J.
121 WOODMONT #13
BOWLING GREEN, KY 42101

DAVIS, JAMES H.
PORTER PAINT CO.
BOX 1439
LOUISVILLE, KY 40201

KENTUCKY

EHRLER, CHARLES D.
1601 TARTAN WAY
LOUISVILLE, KY 40205

FREEMAN, JOHN H.
P.O. BOX 22245
LOUISVILLE, KY 40222

MILLER, JAMES A.
5505 DEA DEA DRIVE
FERN CREEK, KY 40291

OTTE, FRANK G.
RTE 2 — BOX 332 AIKEN RD.
ANCHORAGE, KY 40223

SCHOO, OLLIE J.
201 CARDINAL AVE.
VERSAILLES, KY 40383

SPALDING, PATRICK R.
4504 SANTA PAULA
LOUISVILLE, KY 40219

THOMPSON, JAMES
6600 RIVER RD.
HARRODS CREEK, KY 40027

LOUISIANA

MUNGER, DAVID J.
P.O. BOX 53324
LAFAYETTE, LA 70505

MARYLAND

BRANDT, JR., JEREMIAH M.
20 MARBURY RD.
SEVERNA PARK, MD 21146

COHN, MICHAEL L.
200 SECOND AVE. SE
GLEN BURNIE, MD 21061

DYER, ALLEN R.
6340 FREDERICK RD.
BALTIMORE, MD 21228

DYER, TAMARA A.
6340 FREDERICK RD.
BALTIMORE, MD 21228

HAMILTON, JR., GLADEN R.
182 SOUTHDOWN RD.
EDGEWATER, MD 21037

HORROCKS, HENRY H. "REDS"
1307 LEE LANE
SYKESVILLE, MD 21784

HORROCKS, JEFF
NEVERMORE BALLOON SALES
18245 LOST KNIFE CIRCLE #102
GAITHERSBURG, MD 20760

JANZEN, GEORGE
14812 MARLIN TR.
ROCKVILLE, MD 20853

SAUNDERS, THOMAS A.
205 JUNIPER DR.
GLEN BURNIE, MD 21061

SCHILLER, JIM
10 RIGGS ROAD
SEVERNA PARK, MD 21146

TIPTON, SR., CHARLES A.
8154 FOREST GLEN DR.
PASEDENA, MD 21122

WAGONER, DAVID
24 KELLINGTON DR.
PASADENA, MD 21122

Dr. Norman Cohen's Shrine Balloon

MASSACHUSETTS

GUSS, DANIEL B.
P.O. BOX 27
W. STOCKBRIDGE, MA 01266

HALL, RALPH H.
1656 MASSACHUSETTS AVE.
LEXINTON, MA 02173

ROBINSON, RON
97 NEWELL HILL RD.
STERLING JCT, MA 01565

THOMAS, M.D., CLAYTON L.
DINGLEY DELL
PALMER, MA 01069

THOMAS, WENDY L.
DINGLEY DELL BALLOON PORT
FRT #1
PALMER, MA 01069

WOOD, ROBERT S.
P.O. BOX 281
CONCORD, MA 01742

MICHIGAN

BOYER, THOMAS S.
1813 BRENTWOOD DR.
TROY, MI 48084

CENTERS, RONALD L.
301 SOUTH 5TH ST.
GRAND HAVEN, MI 49417

CHAPMAN, EDWARD J.
5825 PLEASANT LAKE RD.
ANN ARBOR, MI 48103

COMSTOCK, BRUCE PHILLIP
3600 ELIZABETH RD.
ANN ARBOR, MI 48103

COMSTOCK, TUCKER P.
3600 ELIZABETH RD.
ANN ARBOR, MI 48103

DOERING, MAX H.
6300 WHITNEYVILLE RD.
ALTO, MI 49302

FLODEN, ANDREA Z.
12410 WOODHULL LANDING
FENTON, MI 48430

FLODEN, DENNIS E.
BOX 3039
FLINT, MI 48502

FOLEY, WILLIAM D.
11160 N. LINDEN RD.
CLIO, MI 48420

GAUTHIER, THEODORE E.
1926 WOODLAND
SYLVAN LAKE, MI 48053

GRABB, DAVID W.
325 BARTON SHORE DR.
ANN ARBOR, MI 48105

GRABB, WILLIAM CLARENCE
325 BARTON SHORE DR.
ANN ARBOR, MI 48105

GRAHAM, RICH
9520 W. MILO RD.
PLAINWELL, MI 49080

MICHIGAN

HERALD, DAN
403 N. MERCANTILE
CARSON CITY, MI 48811

LAMBECK, ROBERT N.
16619 WINDERMERE CIRCLE
SOUTHGATE, MI 48195

NEVERDAUSKY, JACK D.
2483 SEBASTIAN DR.
GRAND BLANC, MI 48439

PIOTROWSKI, JOHN L.
712 LABADIE CT.
ROCHESTER, MI 48063

SEIDLER, ROBERT E.
1109 WARD
OWOSSO, MI 48867

TKACHIK, SUSAN C.
P.O. BOX 597
WARREN, MI 48090

VANDER HORST, W H M J
2446 E. REID RD.
GRAND BLANC, MI 48439

WARREN, WAYNE
7285 BLUEWATER APT 43
CLARKSTON, MI 48016

WISELY, ROB
4375 PLEASANT LAKE RD.
ANN ARBOR, MI 48104

WOFLSON, MARILYN M.
3000 SEMINOLE
DETROIT, MI 48214

MINNESOTA

ALBERS, GEORGE
1182 SEMINOUG
WGST ST. PAUL, MN 55118

BAIER, LAWRENCE E.
3566 LOWELL ST.
DEEPHAVEN, MN 55391

BONINE, STEVEN J.
3000 ATWOOD DR.
MINNETONKA, MN 55343

LE MAY, STEVE
991 OAKDALE AVE.
WEST ST. PAUL, MN 55118

MICHELS, BOB
1924 JULIET AVENUE
ST. PAUL, MN 55105

PICCARD, THE REV. JEANETTE,
PhD., D.D.
1445 E. RIVER RD.
MINNEAPOLIS, MN 55414

WIEDERKEHR, DENISE
1604 EUCLID STREET
ST. PAUL, MN 55106

WIEDERKEHR, DONNA
1604 EUCLID STREET
ST. PAUL, MN 55106

WIEDERKEHR, MATT H.
1604 EUCLID STREET
ST. PAUL, MN 55106

No book on ballooning would be complete without a photo of gas balloons!

Photo submitted by Tucker Comstock

MISSISSIPPI

BAGLEY, JERRY
RTE 2 — BOX 307B
JACKSON, MS 39209

JENNINGS, JOHN WILLIAM JR.
HOT AIR BALLOONS INC.
#5 PECAN LANE
GREENWOOD, MS 38930

MISSOURI

BACON, DUANE E.
821 ORCHARD
LEES SUMMIT, MO 64063

BARAD, LEONARD M.
28 WILLOW HILL RD.
ST. LOUIS, MO 63124

CAPLAN, DONALD S.
9901 CONWAY RD.
ST. LOUIS, MO 63124

CAPLAN, NIKKI J.
9901 CONWAY RD.
ST. LOUIS, MO 63124

EISENBERG, LEO
1226 W. 64TH ST. TERR.
KANSAS CITY, MO 64113

GATSCHET, C.W.
ROUTE #1, BOX 211
WESTON, MO 64098

GUSTAD, ROBERT W.
1038 SO. FREMONT
SPRINGFIELD, MO 65804

LEDBETTER, MICHAEL S.
14 GARDEN LANE
ST. LOUIS, MO 63122

MORROW, JOYCE E.
147 SOUTH JEWELL
LIBERTY, MO 64068

NEWBURGER, MICHAEL
301 N. SHORE DR.
PARKVILLE, MO 64151

PRESLEY, H.G.
415 COLE ST.
SIKESTON, MO 63801

ROTE, TOM D.
1111 WALNUT ST.
COLUMBIA, MO 65201

SARNO, DONALD A.
68 MORWOOD LANE
ST. LOUIS, MO 63141

SCHETTLER, DANIEL R.
9568 PARKLANE
ST. LOUIS, MO 63124

SINES, GARY DEE
535 S. CRANE
INDEPENDENCE, MO 64050

SINES, JANICE
535 SO. CRANE
INDEPENDENCE, MO 64050

SPAIN, H. DUSTY
7401 N.W. KERNS RD.
KANSAS CITY, MO 64152

MISSOURI

STALEY, EDWARD W.
1534 MASON VALLEY RD.
ST. LOUIS, MO 63131

VAN TOL, LAWRENCE C.
700 SGMINOLE
INDEPENDENCE, MO 64056

WOODARD, TED G.
2727 MAIN
KANSAS CITY, MO 64108

MONTANA

BARROW, THOMAS A.
733 HIGHLAND PARK DR.
BILLINGS, MT 59102

NEBRASKA

ALFRED, MARY JO
RT 2
AXTELL, NE 68924

COOK, CHARLES W.
11303 OAKLAND DR., RR 21
OMAHA, NE 68133

DUNCAN, J. ROBERT
14TH — HILLTOP RD.
LINCOLN, NE 68521

GLOSHEN, DONNA R.
GLOSHEN BALLOONS INC.
1226 N. 121ST ST.
OMAHA, NE 68154

MAHONEY, EARL G.
1120 S. 61ST ST.
OMAHA, NE 68106

MAHONEY, WILLIAM R.
1120 S. 61ST ST.
OMAHA, NE 69341

MASEK, JOE
STAR RTE, BOX 40-A-25
GERING, NE 69341

RAKER, JAMES J.
3503 JONES
OMAHA, NE 68100

WEMHOFF, WILLIAM G.
970 S. 150TH ST.
OMAHA, NE 68154

WHITE, CHERYL
13229 GLENN ST.
PAPILLION, NE 68046

WHITE, RICHARD
13229 GLENN ST.
PAPILLION, NE 68046

WOLDT, WAYNE E.
317 MORTON RD.
COLUMBUS, NE 68601

WOLDT, WILLARD E.
317 MORTON RD.
COLUMBUS, NE 68601

NEVADA

BUSSE, WILLIAM G.
4409 MAYFLOWER LANE
LAS VEGAS, NV 89107

NEVADA

TWEDT, CARTER
500 W. TELEGRAPH ST.
CARSON CITY, NV 89701

TWEDT, MARGARET A.
500 W. TELEGRAPH ST.
CARSON CITY, NV 89701

NEW HAMPSHIRE

MAGNOR, CLIFFORD E.
P.O. BOX 1067
NASHUA, NH 03061

NEW JERSEY

BLAIR, JOHN C.
36 LAKE ST.
BRIDGETON, NJ 08302

BRODY, AARON L.
20 CHESTER RD.
UPPER MT. CLAIR, NJ 07043

CAREY, GRACE
27 SEDGWICK LANE
WILLINGBORO, NJ 08046

EMER, ALLEN R.
7 BROADWAY
OCEAN GROVE, NJ 07756

FLECK, DENNIS M.
BOX 99, HOLLAND RD.
FAR HILLS, NJ 07931

FOGEL, EDWARD G.
747 VALLEY ST.
MAPLEWOOD, NJ 07040

GLYNN, JOSEPH F.
9 S. NEWARK AVE.
VENTNOR, NJ 08406

GRINTON, JOHN M.
276 POTTERSTOWN RD.
LEBANON, NJ 08833

HOEBEL, BART
BRAIN RESEARCH INSTR. CO.
207 HARTLEY AVE.
PRINCETON, NJ 08540

JACOB, FRED
118 LIBERTY CORNER RD.
WARREN, NJ 07060

LA FERA, JOSEPH
48 N. 10TH ST.
NEWARK, NJ 07107

LEWIS, GARY M.
44 HILLCREST BLVD.
WARREN, NJ 07060

LOWE, DAVID E.
WINDRIFTERS, INC.
2 WYCOMBE WAY
PRINCETON JCT., NJ 08550

MICHALSKI, RICHARD K.
10 HARTE PL.
PISCATAWAY, NJ 08854

SMITH, HARRIS FREDERIC
BOX 41 RD 1
CALIFON, NJ 07830

NEW MEXICO

ABRUZZO, BEN L.
9 SANDIN HGTS DR.
ALBUQUERQUE, NM 87122

AMUNDSON, FLOYD A.
7316 CARRIAGE NE
ALBUQUERQUE, NM 87109

BABINGTON, WILLIAM R.
7408 EUCLID NE
ALBUQUERQUE, NM 87110

BACHTELL, SHERI
3413 YOSEMITE NE
ALBUQUERQUE, NM 87111

BENNETT, CLAIR E.
P.O. BOX 1499
FARMINGTON, NM 87401

BENSON, DR. ROBERT W.
1009 GUADALUPE DEL PRUDO
ALBUQUERQUE, NM 87107

BOOK, C. WARREN (WALLY)
1011 JACKSON, S.E.
ALBUQUERQUE, NM 87108

BROWN, RICHARD M.
EDITOR, BALLOONING
2516 HIAWATHA DR. NE
ALBUQUERQUE, NM 87112

CARTER, SAMUEL R.
10601 MENAUL NE
ALBUQUERQUE, NM 87112

COOK, KENNETH W.
1105 CUATRO CERROS TR SE
ALBUQUERQUE, NM 87123

CROSBY, JAMES R.
1905 SHIRANE NE
ALBUQUERQUE, NM 87112

DAVIS, CAROL R.
1312 LOS ARBOLES AVE.
ALBUQUERQUE, NM 87107

DAVIS IV, JOHN C.
1312 LOS ARBOLES AVE. NW
ALBUQUERQUE, NM 87107

DAWSON, ROBERT M.
7501 GLADDEN AVE. NE
ALBUQUERQUE, NM 87110

DOUGLAS, BILL G.
2525 ZEARING N.W.
ALBUQUERQUE, NM 87104

FARR, FREDERICK A.
12104 MANITOBA NE
ALBUQUERQUE, NM 87111

FARR, TRUDY R.
12104 MANITOBA NE
ALBUQUERQUE, NM 87111

FLYNT II, BILL W.
111 E. 22ND ST. APT. 101
ROSWELL, NM 88201

FOUTZ, GARY A.
1809 E. NAVAJO
FARMINGTON, NM 87401

GIBBS, BRAD E.
4822 IDLEWILDE LANE SE
ALBUQUERQUE, NM 87108

A typical balloon scene submitted by Charles Platt of Illinois. Balloon is a Piccard. Note how shape of gores vary from one manufacturer to another.

NEW MEXICO

GLEN, WILLIAM S.
67 LUEBKE PLACE
ROSWELL, NM 88201

GOTTLIEB, KURT
P.O. BOX 67
CUBERO, NM 87014

GUNTER, DARRYL R.
114 HERMOSA SE
ALBUQUERQUE, NM 87108

HARRISON, LANGDON D.
7311 MONTGOMERY NE
BOX H190
ALBUQUERQUE, NM 87109

HESS, STEPHEN G.
4310 PAN AM HWY NE 211
ALBUQUERQUE, NM 87107

HINKLE II, ROLLA R.
1213 WEST 3RD
ROSWELL, NM 88201

JOHN, ROBERT G.
1413 GEORGIA NE
ALBUQUERQUE, NM 87110

KINNEY, CHARLOTTE JEAN
3006 VISTA GRANDE NW
ALBUQUERQUE, NM 87120

KMATZ, MICHAEL J.
7512 VISTA DEL ARROYO NE
ALBUQUERQUE, NM 87109

MARCH, CONNIE L.
6905 HENSCH NE
ALBUQUERQUE, NM 87109

MARCH, DOUGLAS B.
6905 HENSCH NE
ALBUQUERQUE, NM 87109

MC CONNELL, THOMAS S.
1742 DIETZ PLACE NW
ALBUQUERQUE, NM 87107

NEWITT, GLENN
609 E. ISLETA
FARMINGTON, NM 87401

O BRIEN, PAULA Z.
520 LOS RANCHOS NW
ALBUQUERQUE, NM 87107

PICKARD, PAULA J.
BOX 1499
FARMINGTON, NM 87401

RAY, CHARELS W.
1036 FLORIDA SE
ALBUQUERQUE, NM 87108

RAY, KEITH J.
1036 FLORIDA SE
ALBUQUERQUE, NM 87108

RUSSELL, ROBERT E.
P.O. BOX 8005
ALBUQUERQUE, NM 87108

SLONAKER, RONALD E.
2626 N. DUSTIN APT. 28
FARMINGTON, NM 87401

TOLES, J. PENROD
P.O. BOX 1300
ROSWELL, NM 88201

NEW MEXICO

WHITLOW, JERRY R.
307 REESE NE
ALBUQUERQUE, NM 87107

WILSON, GREG
804 MAXINE NE
ALBUQUERQUE, NM 87123

WILSON, MARK
P.O. BOX 25181
ALBUQUERQUE, NM 87112

ZANOTTI, THOMAS P.
2212 LESTER DR., N.E. #435
ALBUQUERQUE, NM 87112

NEW YORK

ARMSTRONG, JR., WILLIAM G.
#1 WASHINGTON SQUARE
VILLAGE
APT I-13
NEW YORK, NY 10012

AUCHINCLOSS, ROBERT G.
152 COLLEGE AVE.
POUGHKEEPSIE, NY 12602

BARBER, RUSSELL L.
P.O. BOX 316
NIVERVILLE, NY 12130

BOMBARD, BUDDY
42 TANGLEWYLDE AVE.
BRONXVILLE, NY 10708

COLLIN, VICTOR W.
P.O. BOX 102-AMF
JFK INT'L AIRPORT
JAMAICA, NY 11430

DES JARDINS, JOHN
211 E. 73rd STREET
NEW YORK, NY 10021

EDWARDS, RONALD W.
611 BUTTON RD.
CHITTENANGO, NY 13037

EORMAN, JOEY
THE WIND GYPSIES
P.O. BOX 234
WATERVLIET, NY 12189

FORBES, MALCOLM S.
FORBES MAGAZINE
60 FIFTH AVE.
NEW YORK, NY 10011

HUGHES, WILLIAM D.
RT 4-BOS 246 MOUNTAIN RD
PLEASANT VALLEY, NY 12569

JACKSON, PHIL
462 GLEN ST.
GLENS FALLS, NY 12801

KELLY, PETER J.
169 FULTON AVE.
CENTRAL SQUARE, NY 13036

KENNETT, BOBBIE
230 NYAC AVE.
PELHAM, NY 10803

LANDON, P. CRAIG, LCDR, USN
VA 66
FPO, NY 09501

LEWIS, DR. GEORGE T.
BOX 536
HUGHSONVILLE, NY 12537

NEW YORK

MEGARO, ALICE
21 WILDCLIFF RD.
NEW ROCHELLE, NY 10805

MEUER, ANN
301 E. 62ND ST.
NEW YORK, NY 10021

MURRAY, KENNETH P.
P.O. BOX 190
SHENOROCK, NY 10587

POMEROY, RICK J.
USBER (BASC)
BERLIN, GERMANY
A.P.O., NY 09742

REPAK, HARRY J.
BOX 171 LGA AIRPORT STA.
FLUSHING, NY 11371

SALZBERG, RUTH F.
11 TAYLOR RD.
ELMSFORD, NY 10523

SCHWENKER, RUDOLPH C.
81 CEDAR AVE.
POUGHKEEPSIE, NY 12603

STAR BALLOONS
STEVEN, DAVID S.
BOX 6 — BELINGROVE MANOR
VALATIE, NY 12184

SUTHERLAND, JAMES S.
75 MARTIN DR.
POUGHKEEPSIE, NY 12603

TEITSWORTH, CARROLL G.
BARBER HILL RD.
GROVELAND, NY 14462

ZUCZUSKI, RAYMOND F.
5 SO. LYON ST.
BATAVIA, NY 14020

NORTH CAROLINA

BLEVINS, BILL
P.O. BOX 26
SCOTTS, NC 28699

CLINE, J. DONALD
807 LARKWOOD DR.
GREENSBORO, NC 27410

KNIGHT, JAMES T. III
RTE 4 BOX 255
STATESVILLE, NC 28677

LITTLE, DAVID N.
P.O. BOX 1304
CONCORD, NC 28025

MEDDOCK, DODDS
RHYNE AERODOME RFD 2
STATESVILLE, NC 28677

MICHAEL, HOWARD M.
P.O. BOX 1236
LINCOLNTON, NC 28092

SCHOO, JANET L.
1930 ELIZABETH AVE. #2
WINSTON-SALEM, NC 27103

SIMPSON, WELDON
P.O. BOX 746
JACKSONVILLE, NC 28540

Author learning some of the pitfalls . . . or rather, "swampfalls" of ballooning. Aerostat is a Raven S50-A owned by Kingswood Sprott of Lakeland, Florida.

Photo Courtesy NEWS-CHIEF

NORTH CAROLINA

WENZ, EMILY D.
RT. II, BOX 279
STATESVILLE, NC 28677

WENZ, GEORGE R.
RT. 11, BOX 279
STATESVILLE, NC 28677

WOOLLEY, PORTIS
RTE 11 — BOX 279
STATESVILLE, NC 28677

OHIO

BARNUM, ERIC E.
228 W. BROADWAY
MAUMEE, OH 43537

CONTOS, JIM
443 LINDENWOOD AVE.
AKRON, OH 44301

DRISCOLL, DENIS B.
11600 WILTS LANE
MEDWAY, OH 45341

FREY, JAMES R.
1490 S. CLINTON ST.
DEFIANCE, OH 43512

HAWKINS, JOHN C.
226 E. MICHIGAN ST.
SEBRING, OH 44672

JACKSON, JAMES M.
4622 COACH RD.
COLUMBUS, OH 43220

LAPPIES, EDWARD R.
7745 LAKESHORE BLVD.
N. MADISON, OH 44057

LITTER, MARK W.
RTE 9
CHILLICOTHE, OH 45601

MEDDOCK, GARY A.
2401 BRAHMS
DAYTON, OH 45449

MEDDOCK, MARSHA R.
2401 BRAHMS, BLVD.
DAYTON, OH 45449

NEWHOUSE, BUD
817 WEYMOUTH CT.
CINCINNATI, OH 45240

O'LONE, RANDI L.
237 S. LAKEVIEW DR.
MILLBURY, OH 43447

SABO, JAMES M.
80 GREENWOOD
RITTMAN, OH 44270

SCHOFIELD, DONALD W.
2863 ZOLTINGER RD.
UPPER ARLINGTON, OH 43221

STEWART, RONALD B.
576 D'LYN DR.
COLUMBUS, OH 43228

SULZBACH, BEVERLY L.
639 PARKWAY BLVD.
NORTON, OH 44203

OHIO

SWANSON, ARTHUR H.
38 FERGUSON DR.
TALLMADGE, OH 44278

THOMSON, BLAKE A.
21 AUDUBON LANE
POLAND, OH 44514

WELLS, JOHN A.
830 FAIRVIEW AVE.
BARBERTON, OH 44203

ZANELLA, ROBERT L.
220 — 2ND ST. NW
BARBERTON, OH 44203

OKLAHOMA

MAXWELL, ROBERT N.
612 PINE TREE RD.
FREDERICK, OK 73542

OREGON

ETZEL, SPENCER G.
2215 CLAXTER RD.
SALEM, OR 97303

PENNSLYVANIA

ADKINS, RAY
R.D. #1
WAYNESBORO, PA 17268

BERNICK, SHELDON M.
110 MARTINS RUN
MEDIA, PA 19151

DONAVEN, JAMES D.
378 WOODLAND VIEW DR.
YORK, PA 17402

DULL, JEFFRY
APT B-5 BAUGHMAN HALL
LUTHERAN THEOLOGICAL SEMINARY
GETTYSBURG, PA 17325

FAIRBANKS, ANTHONY MEAD
113 MICHIGAN AVE.
SWATHMORE, PA 19081

FISHER, JOE M.
RR 2 — BOX 254
CHAMBERBURG, PA 17201

FORTE, TIMOTHY P.
264 HENLEY RD.
PHILADELPHIA, PA 19151

GABLE, H.E. & PETE
2735 GRANDVIEW AVE.
YORK, PA 17404

HESS, RICHARD F.
BOX 311 — RTE 2
MOUNT JOY, PA 17552

LEWIS, MAURICE J. MD
TWO CAMPBELL PLACE
CAMP HILL, PA 17011

MC CLINTIC, FRED E.
810 STRATFORD DR. #9
STATE COLLEGE, PA 16801

G-OLLI! A most appropriate registration.

Courtesy Cameron Balloons

PENNSLYVANIA

MILLER, JR., DR. EDGAR R.
OLD KENNETT RD.
KENNETH SQUARE, PA 19348

NEIMER, JOHN
P.O. BOX 4
BOILING SPRINGS, PA 17007

POWELL, CHRISTOPHER J.
3200 BIRNEY AVE.
SCRANTON, PA 18505

POWELL, JOHN D.
3200 BIRNEY AVE.
SCRANTON, PA 18505

POWELL, RICHARD
38 2-B CROWN CIRCLE DRIVE
SCRANTON, PA 18505

SWARTLEY, COLLEEN E.
726 N. 2nd ST.
STEELTON, PA. 17113

TATE, JOHN R.
9 DIANI DR.
MALVERN, PA 19355

SOUTH DAKOTA

BOOTH, STEVEN DALE
721 S. PHILLIPS AVE.
SIOUX FALLS, SD 57102

DURSTON, STAN C.
416 S. POLK
PIERRE, SD 57501

MOQUIST, RONALD M.
2001 ELIZABETH DR.
SIOUX FALLS, SD 57103

OLIVIER, ORVIN E.
709 S. BAHNSON AVE.
SIOUX FALLS, SD 57103

ULVESTAD, DENNIS K.
5200 WEST 37TH
SIOUX FALLS, SD 57106

WINKER, GREG J.
2805 POPLAR DR.
SIOUX FALLS, SD 57105

TENNESSEE

EASTLAND, DAVID C.
RTE 8
FRANKLIN, TN 37064

GABLE, LINDA
P.O. BOX 9
LOOK-OUT MOUNTAIN, TN 37350

GABEL, TOM
GABLE BALLOON FIELD
P.O. BOX 9
LOOK-OUT MOUNTAIN, TN 37350

JARMAN, FRANKLIN M.
FIRST AMERICAN CENTER
NASHVILLE, TN 37328

PARKER, WILLIAM D.
769 LANOIR ST.
CHATTANOOGA, TN 37412

TENNESSEE

SOESBE, ERIC L.
LAKEWOOD DR.
TULLAHOMA, TN 37388

STAMPS, CLARENCE JR.
300 BAKERTOWN RD #20
ANTIOCH, TN 37013

WINSETT, O.W.
3420 PHILSDALE AVE.
MEMPHIS, TN 38111

WINSETT & LEACH INC.
2910 SOUTHWAY DR.
MEMPHIS, TN 38118

TEXAS

ALLISON, BARRETT D.
12935 WESTLIEGH
HOUSTON, TX 77077

BAILEY, DAVID W.
917 TUSING AVE.
GRAND PRAIRIE, TX 75050

COMPTON, JOHN M.
BOX 623
MISSION, TX 78572

CONEWAY, R. PAUL
BOX 805
HEREFORD, TX 79045

COOPER, TERRY J.
400 E. 3RD ST.
TYLER, TX 75701

DOEHRING, DAN E.
2822 DURBAN DR.
HOUSTON, TX 77043

DUGAS, PAUL R.
7727 SHADYVILLA #25
HOUSTON, TX 77055

EDWARDS, SAM B.
14906 BRAMBLEWOOD
HOUSTON, TX 77079

FILIP, RICHARD J.
2014 WROXTON RD.
HOUSTON, TX 77005

GARGOTTA, MARY E.
1281 BLALOCK
HOUSTON, TX 77055

HARDIN, WILLIAM T.
7631 RAMBLER RD. APT. 164
DALLAS, TX 75231

HEWITT, RALPH
724 INTERNATIONAL BLVD
F-36
HOUSTON, TX 77024

JONES, CLIFFORD DALE
2105 N. PENELOPE
BELTON, TX 76513

JONES, GEORGE W.
6360 SKYLINE #28
HOUSTON, TX 77057

KERLEY, EDDIE R.
1828 PETROLEUM
ODESSA, TX 79760

LONG, RONNY W.
3414 E. MAIN ST.
GRAND PRAIRIE, TX 75050

MC COLLUM JR., L. FRANK
P.O. BOX 500
HOUSTON, TX 77001

TEXAS

MC DONALD, MD., HENRY C.
6709 BRANTS LANE
FT. WORTH, TX 76116

MEADOR, J.C.
218 E. EDGEBROOK
HOUSTON, TX 77034

MURTORFF, WILLIAM C.
RAINBOWS END BALLOON PRT
7826 FAIRVIEW
HOUSTON, TX 77041

PATTON, FORREST H.
807 BRIARPARK
HOUSTON, TX 77042

PEGRAM, ROBERT B.
3039 ANZIO
DALLAS, TX 75224

RANDOLF, RONALD D.
P.O. BOX 352
TAFT, TX 78390

ROSS, ED
7630 DEL MONTE
HOUSTON, TX 77063

SCHENDEL, ROBERT T.
2001 BRANARD #6
HOUSTON, TX 77098

THOMPSON, KEVIN F.
913 TUSING AVE.
GRAND PRAIRIE, TX 75050

VAN KIRK, RODNEY W.
447 DE SOTO DRIVE
UNIVERSAL CITY, TX 78148

WEAVER, JAMES W.
9329 GREENSWARD
HOUSTON, TX 77080

WEEMS, KEITH D.
P.O. BOX 614
GRAND PRAIRIE, TX 75051

WEILER, DONALD R.
8700 WOODWAY #129
HOUSTON, TX 77063

UTAH

HANSELL, JEFF T.
2312 WALKER LANE
SALT LAKE CITY, UT 84117

HARRISON, COURTNEY
33 S. WOLCOTT
SALT LAKE CITY, UT 84102

SEYMOUR, ANTHONY C.
5003 WALLACE LANE
SALT LAKE, UT 84117

VIRGINIA

DENNIS, CHIP
3608 SHERWOOD PL.
LYNCHBURG, VA 24503

GODDARD, NEIL W., CWO-4
QTRS 4039-B, MCB
QUANTICO, VA 22134

VIRGINIA

HENDERSON, WALLACE D.
3408 N. EMERSON
ARLINGTON, VA 22207

KNIGHT, JOSEPH S. JR.
BOX 1352
MIDDLEBURG, VA 22117

KOHLER, MICHAEL J.
11010 BRISTOW RD.
BRISTOW, VA 22013

MICHAELS, R. PATRICK
5500 HOLMES RUN PKWY. 503
ALEXANDRIA, VA 22304

MISTELE, WILLIAM HENRY
1309 BISCAYNE RD.
HOLLINS, VA 24019

PATTERSON, MICHAEL
104 EASTLAWN DR.
HAMPTON, VA 23664

POLIZZI, GARY S.
3409 JOHN MARSHALL DR.
ARLINGTON, VA 22207

ROSE, ROBERT E.
2205 GRAYSON PL.
FALLS CHURCH, VA 22043

THOMPSON, FRANK R.
3330 N. WASHINGTON BLVD.
ARLINGTON, VA 22201

TYCHSEN, JR., PAUL E.
6935 HAYCOCK RD.
FALLS CHURCH, VA 22043

WASHINGTON

HOWARD, PHILIP S.
5511 W. SAMMAMISH RD. N.
REDMOND, WA 98052

LLOYD, BILL
1440 S. 3RD
WALLA WALLA, WA 99362

VALE, VIRGINIA L.
690 COUNTRY CLUB RD.
WALLA WALLA, WA 99362

VANIK, MEL F.
64 CASCADE KEY
BELLEVUE, WA 98006

WALTER, FOREY L.
S 4323 LOCUST RD.
SPOKANE, WA 99206

WEST VIRGINIA

LANTZ, LARRY O.
RTE 3 — BOX 143
BRIDGEPORT, WV 26330

WISCONSIN

BAKKER, DIRK G.
5149 N. WOODBURN
MILWAUKEE, WI 53217

BEGER, ROBERT K.
10701 W. NORTH AVE.
MILWAUKEE, WI 53226

Wil holding crown line in a less common view of a hot air balloon.

WISCONSIN

BOEDE, ROBERT
6375 DOWLING RD.
OMRO, WI 54963

BRITTON, GARY L.
3875 SCHUSTER DR.
WEST BEND, WI 53095

DEHN, RICHARD W.
406 PALMER AVE.
GREEN LAKE, WI 54947

FONTAINE, MICHAEL A.
208 W. MILLER ST.
GREENWOOD, WI 54437

GRAVES, HAROLD C.
P.O. BOX 25243
MILWAUKEE, WI 53225

KADONSKY, STEVE J.
5010 N. 91ST ST.
MILWAUKEE, WI 53221

MITTELSTADT, GLENN O.
RTE 2 — BOX 261
CAMPBELLSPORT, WI 53010

SHEPPARD, THOMAS A.F.
1232 HAWTHORNE DR.
WEST BEND, WI 53095

SPAETH, DAWN J.
N168 W21058 MAIN ST.
JACKSON, WI 53037

SPAETH, DEBBRA A.
N168W21058 MAIN ST.
JACKSON, WI 53037

SWARTZ, JOHN C.
1706 PRAIRIE RD.
MADISON, WI 53711

VANDENBERG, RONALD V.
616 HARRISON
LITTLE CHUTE, WI 54140

WRIGHT, JAMES R.
3110 SOUTH 27th ST.
LA CROSSE, WI 54601

WORLD PILOTS

EXCEPT UNITED STATES OF AMERICA

Ballooning "down under",
Dunedin, New Zealand.
A beautiful Cameron owned by
[illegible] Lloyd.

ALBERTA FREE BALLOONIST SOCIETY
P.O. BOX 6897 — STA D
CALGARY, AB
CANADA T2P 2G1

ALLEN, RICHARD
14 BINSCARTH ROAD
TORONTO, ONTARIO
CANADA M4W 1Y1

BADER, RUTH
FUGGERSTR 3
D8901 LETTERSHOFEN
AUGSBURG, GERMANY

BALKEDAL, JAN G.C.
GEIJERSGATAN 57
75231 UPPSALA
SWEDEN

BALLOONING CLUB OF INDIA
SAFDARJUNG AIRPORT
NEW DELI 110003
INDIA

BARKER, DAVID
ASONS LIN
ANES ROAD
AWBRIDGE
ROMSEY
HANTS. SO5 OHL
ENGLAND

BARNES, FRANK
9, CHADWELL HEATH LANE
CHADWELL HEATH,
ESSEX
ENGLAND

BAUMAN, JOHN M.
5 GRANDIN VILLAGE
ST. ALBERT, ALBERTA
T8N1R9 CANADA

BOESMAN, NINI
STATENLAAN 2A — THE HAGUE
HOLLAND

BRIDGE, CAPT. MARTIN
CATHAY PACIFIC AIRWAYS
KAI TAK AIRPORT
HONG KONG

BURROW, SRAEME
TASON ST.
DUNEDIN, NEW ZEALAND

CLARIDGE, DAVID
FINCH LANE
LITTLE CHALFONT
BUCKINGHAMSHIRE
ENGLAND

COSTA DE BEAUREGARD JEAN
CHATEN-DE-FONTAINES
77139 ENTREPILLY
FRANCE

DANNERBO, ALFRED
DALSTROGET 146
DK 2860 SOBORG
DENMARK

DE MAREVIL, GILLES
c/o 3 BIS SQUARE A. ARNAUD
75116 PARIS, FRANCE

DE SAINT SAUVEUR
c/o 3 BIS SQUARE A. ARNAUD
75116 PARIS, FRANCE

DE VILLARS, ARNAUD
14 RUE DU MT. VALERIEN
F 92210 ST. CLOUD
FRANCE

DORMAN, ACAN
REST HARROW
WOODLANDS LANE
WINDELSHAM
SURREY
ENGLAND

Joseph Starkbaum of Austria with his invention, the "by-pass burner". He made the first Austria-Yugoslavia alpine crossing.

EDMONTON BALLOON CLUB
BOX 7688 STATION A
EDMONTON, ALBERTA
T5J 2X8 CANADA

EMERING, PAUL
4, RUE DU CIMETIERE
KEHLEN
LUXEMBOURG

FELTS, ALFI
180, RUE CENTS
KALTGESBRUCK
LUXEMBOURG

FLORANDER, DAVID
KIGNAESBAKKEN 16
3630 JAEGERSPRIS, DENMARK

GIANNIOTIS, PAUL
CATHAY PACIFIC AIRWAYS
KAI TAK AIRPORT
HONG KONG

GREEN, CAPT GEOFF
CATHAY PACIFIC AIRWAYS
KAI TAK AIRPORT
HONG KONG

GRUBBSTROM, JOHN A T
BERGSGATAN 7.5 TR
S 73100 KOPINE
SWEDEN

GUPTA, VISHWA B
8B BAHADURSHAH ZAFAR MARG
NEW DELI
INDIA

HASSOLD, HORST
D-8900 AUGSBURG 3
POSTFACH 280
GERMANY

HENNEQUGT, FRANCOIS
c/o 3 BIS SQUARE A. ARNAUD
75116 PARIS, FRANCE

HERRING, BOB
389 PING HALL RD
DUNEDIN, NEW ZEALAND

HISLOP, L.M.C.
P.O. BOX 7104
PALMERSTON NORTH
NEW ZEALAND

HORACK, LARRY J.
306 EUCLID STREET
WHITBY, ONTARIO
CANADA LIN 5B6

HUNNIFORD, BRENT A.
2791 DEWDNEY TRUNK RD.
COQUILTLAN, BC
CANADA

HUNT, DAVID
FASTNET HOUSE
WICKHAM
NR. NEWBURY
BERKS.
ENGLAND

HURRAN, VICTOR
OAK COTTAGE
BAUGHURST
TADLEY
BERKS.
ENGLAND

HVAL, BRIAN H.
1712 HOME ROAD
CALGARY, ALBERTA
CANADA T3B 1G9

ICHIYOSHI, SABURO
3-31-27 MINAMI-OGIKUBO
SUGINAMI-KU TOKYO
167 JAPAN

JENKINSON, ALEC
7 LYTTON GROVE
LONDON SW15 2 EP
ENGLAND

Vishwa Bandhu Gupta, a man of many talents, and India's only licensed balloonist in command of "Udankhatola", which he built.

KATZER, WOLF R.
D 8900 AUGSBURG
POSTFACH 110743
GERMANY

KENNGALLY, RAY
CATHAY PACIFIC AIRWAYS
KAI TAK AIRPORT
HONG KONG

KOSTUR, DANIEL L.
149 MARIA ST.
TORONTO, ONTARIO
CANADA, M6P 1W5

KOSTUR, JERRY
149 MARIA ST.
TORONTO, ONTARIO
CANADA M6P 1W5

LEWIS, NOES
5 ACRES-KILLEGAR
ENNISKERRY-CO WICKLOW
IRELAND

LEWIS-SMITH, MRS. ANNE
MEAD HOUSE
POTSGROVE WOBURN
BEDS MK 17 9HG
ENGLAND

LITTLEWOOD, CHARLOS A.
9141 153 RO ST
GOMONTON, ALBERTA
CANADA T5R 1P5

LLOYD, KEN
P.O. BOX 1223
DUNEDIN, NEW ZEALAND

LOOS, FRIEDEL F.
D-6456 LANGENSELBOLD/HE S
HANAUER STRASSE 20
WEST GERMANY

LOUTHAN, DAVID
ROWCHESTER HOUSE
GREENLAW, (SCOTLAND)
BERWICKSHIRE, U.K.

LUKER, NED
36 LYNDHURST ROAD
JOHANNESBURG 2192
SO. AFRICA

MADSEN, AXEL
S-JOGATAN 41
560 30 GRANNA, SWEDEN

MAHONEY, LT. JAMES D.
PSC BOX 3259
BITBURG, A.B.
GERMANY (A.P.O. N.Y. 09132)

MOBERG, ROLAND B.
35 SILVER RIDGE RISG, N.W.
CALGARY, ALBERTA
CANADA

MORGAN, PETER D. ESQ.
BASSETBURY MILL
BASSETBURY LANE
HIGH WYCOMBE
BUCKINGHAMSHIRE
ENGLAND

MORRISON, PATRICK
APPLE TREE COTTAGE
WILTON,
NR. MARLBOROUGH
WILTS.
ENGLAND

MOSS, STEPHEN
BASEMENT FLAT
41 GRAFTON SQUARE
LONDON SWX
ENGLAND

One of the Cathay Pacific Airways balloons in free flight over Asia.

OGG, GARY
CATHAY PACIFIC AIRWAYS
KAI TAK AIRPORT
HONG KONG

ONESKI, WARNER M.
130 MARWOOD CIRCLE NE
CALGARY, ALBERTA T2A
CANADA

OTAGO BALLOON CLUB INC.
P.O. BOX 1223
DUNEDIN
NEW ZEALAND

PAAMAND, KAI
DK 3600 (GRAESE)
GYVELHOJ
DENMARK

PAAMAND, KIM
DK 3600 (GRAESE)
GYVELHOJ
DENMARK

PETROVICH, DR. ENRIQUE G.
FONT MARTELO 104E
ESQ. SELENIA
HUMACAO, PUERTO RICO

PHOENIX BALLOON CLUB
c/o COVENTRY GLIDING CLUB
HUSBANDS BOSWORTH
NR. LUTTERWORTH
LEICESTERSHIRE
ENGLAND

RAMBOL, AAGE
DK 3600 (GRAESE)
GYVELHOJ
DENMARK

RIHGT, PHILIPPE
c/o 3 BIS SQUARE
A. ARNAUD
75116 PARIS, FRANCE

ROOT, ALAN
BOX 43747
NAIROBI KENYA
E. AFRICA

RUENZI, KURT E.
KUESNACHTERSTR. 59
CH-8126 ZUMINKON-ZURICH
SWITZERLAND

SCHOLZ, CHARLOTTE
27 RENNWEG
8001 ZURICH
SWITZERLAND

SELENKE, GERALD F.
BOX LR 342 TECH-SCHOOL LERIBE
LERIBE, LESOTHO
AFRICA

SELMAN, EDWARD H.
73 DENNING ST.
COOGEE, N.S.W. 2034
AUSTRALIA

SHEROODU BALLOONIST SOCIETY
P.O. BOX 483
RED DEER, ALBERTA
CANADA T4N 5G1

SMITH, BOB
4 SPIERS ROAD
DUNEDIN, NEW ZEALAND

STEEMAN, B.M.
KLEINZAND 25
HOEK VAN HOLLAND
HOLLAND

STARKBAUM, JOSEF
THURNBERG STRASSE 13
A 2346 MA. ENZERSDORF
AUSTRIA

Balloon "Danmark", a Thunder AX-7, and flagship of the Danish Aerostatic Society.

Photo courtesy Kai Paamand

SAUDER, JEAN
54 BD NAPOLEON 1
LUXEMBOURG

TAAFFE, RONALD W.
L1 CLEARWATER BAY APTS
7 MILES CLEARWATER BAY
KOWLOON, HONG KONG

TAKACH, ADAM
CATHAY PACIFIC AIRWAYS
KAI TAK AIRPORT
HONG KONG

THEISEN, VORBERT
63 ROUTE BECHTERNACH
LUXEMBOURG

THIBO, PETE
18 RUE DES ROMAINS
SENNINGERBERT
LUXEMBOURG

THORNE, VICTOR J.
NORWOOD 42 BATH RD.
BRISTOL BS15 6DG
U.K.

TORU, TAKAHASKI
c/o MR. S. HASHIMOTO
2914 KOMAB BEGURO-KU
TOKYO, JAPAN

UNGERMARK, STEVE H.
SLATTERVAGEN 17B
S — 141 70 HUDDINGE
SWEDEN

VILLEY-DESMESERETS, T.
41 RUE DE LEGLISE
75015 PARIS
FRANCE

VISSCHER, G. & W.
2 BORNEDSTRAAT
THE HAGUE
HOLLAND

WILLIAMS, CAPT. T.B.
24 TREBARWITH CRESCENT JAFC, ARAS
NEWQUAY, CORNWALL
ENGLAND

WILLIS, JOHN
c/o 3 BIS SQUARE A. ARNAUD
75116 PARIS
FRANCE

WINDER, DAVID
1 BRANSTREG DRIVE
COVENTRY CV6 6GB
ENGLAND

WOODS, KEN
961 INGRAM CRESCENT
MIDLAND, ONTARIO
CANADA L4R 4E9

Ned Luker of Johannesburg, South Africa lifting a hang-glider with his Thunder 77A.

Photo courtesy Otago Ballooning Club Inc., New Zealand

BALLOON MANUFACTURERS

LISTED ALPHABETICALLY

ADAMS BALLOON LOFT INC.
P.O. BOX 12168
ATLANTA, GEORGIA
U.S.A.

PHONE 404-261-5818

N9008A

AVIAN BALLOON
SOUTH 4323 LOCUST ROAD
SPOKANE, WASHINGTON 99206
U.S.A.

PHONE 509-928-6847

N29616

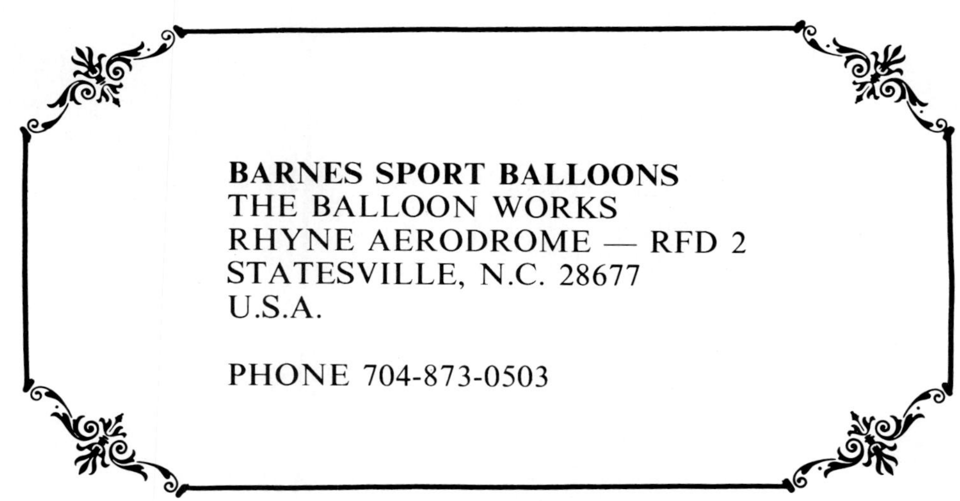
BARNES SPORT BALLOONS
THE BALLOON WORKS
RHYNE AERODROME — RFD 2
STATESVILLE, N.C. 28677
U.S.A.
PHONE 704-873-0503

N2708

* Plan books and construction consultation, not stock balloons.

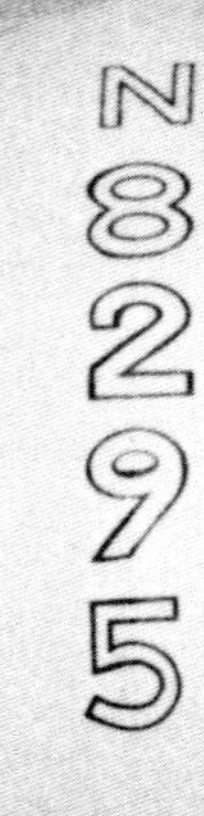
N8295

boland
balloon

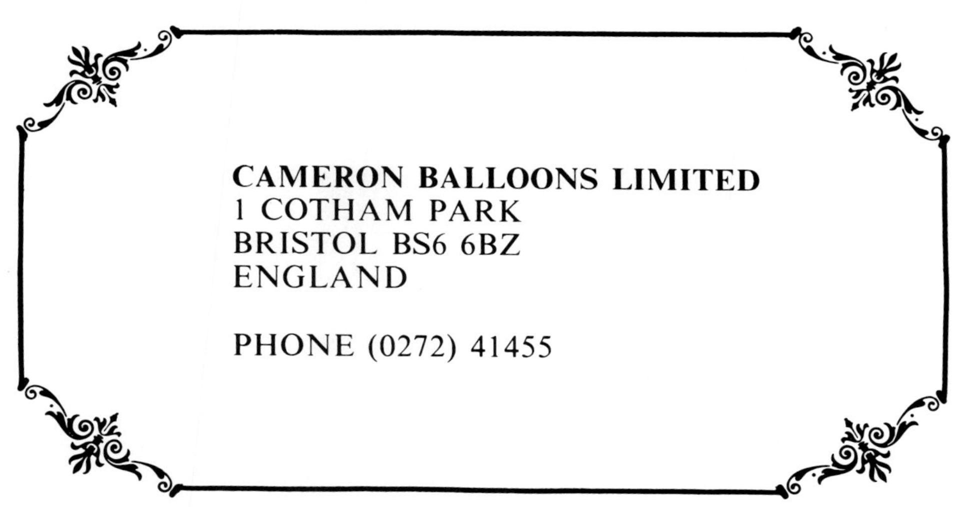

CAMERON BALLOONS LIMITED
1 COTHAM PARK
BRISTOL BS6 6BZ
ENGLAND

PHONE (0272) 41455

Levi's
PH-

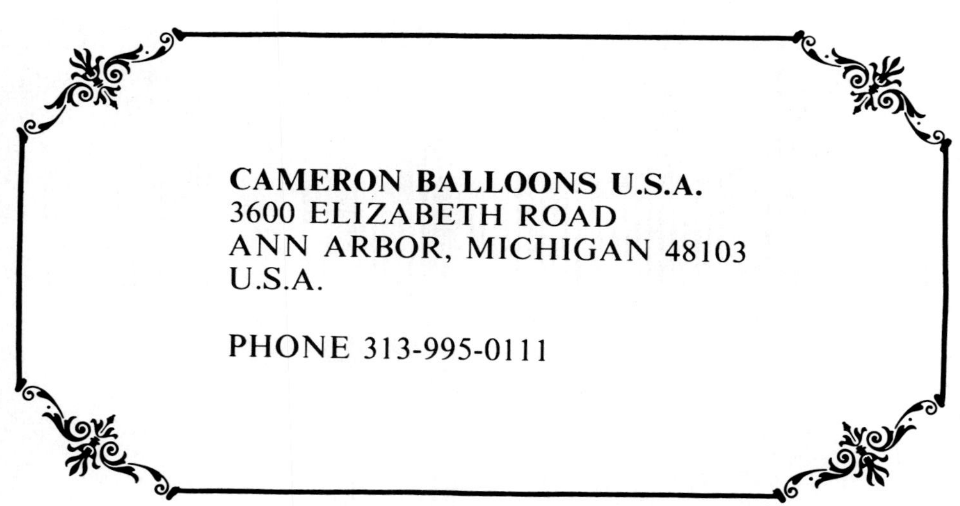

CAMERON BALLOONS U.S.A.
3600 ELIZABETH ROAD
ANN ARBOR, MICHIGAN 48103
U.S.A.

PHONE 313-995-0111

DON PICCARD BALLOONS INC.
P.O. BOX 1902
NEWPORT BEACH, CALIFORNIA 92663
U.S.A.

PHONE 714-642-3545

N5W

RAVEN INDUSTRIES INC.
BOX 1007
SIOUX FALLS, S.D. 57101
U.S.A.

PHONE 605-336-2750

N1032R
Raven

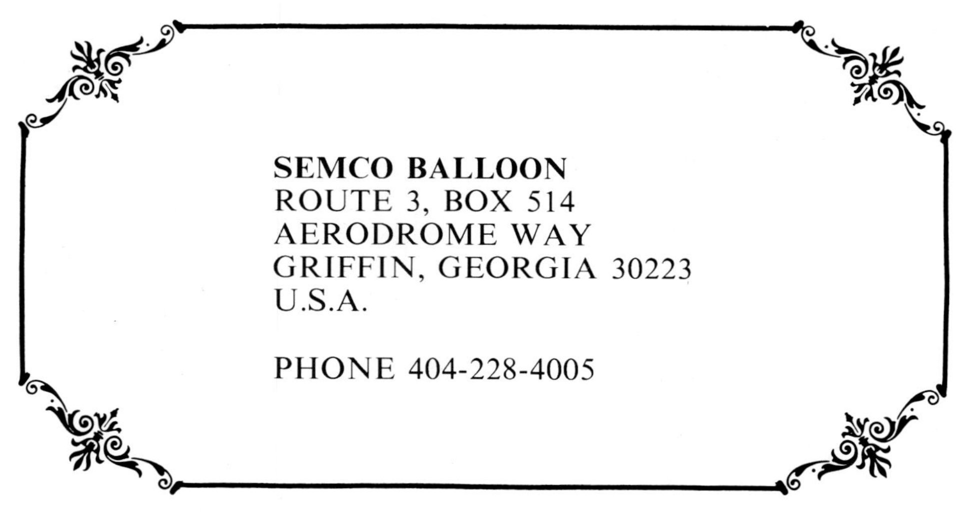
SEMCO BALLOON
ROUTE 3, BOX 514
AERODROME WAY
GRIFFIN, GEORGIA 30223
U.S.A.
PHONE 404-228-4005

N4545
SEMCO

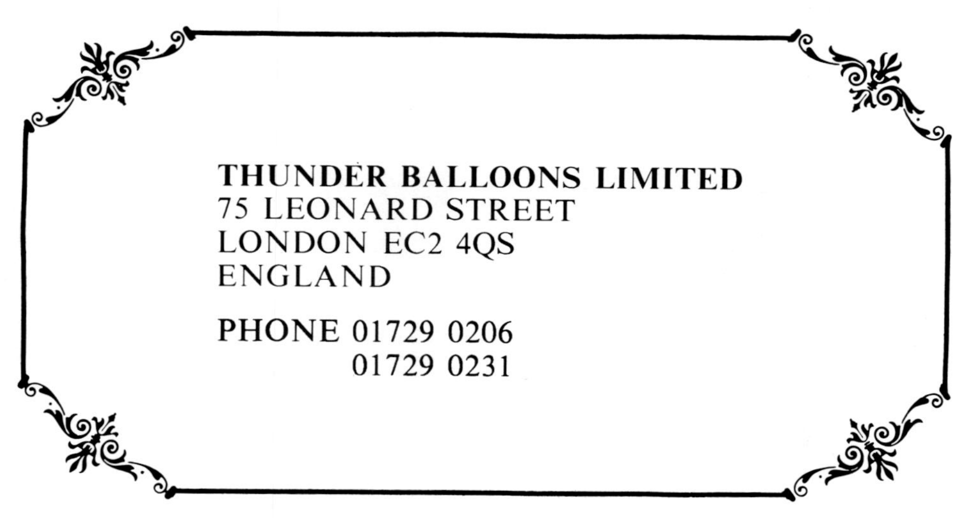

THUNDER BALLOONS LIMITED
75 LEONARD STREET
LONDON EC2 4QS
ENGLAND

PHONE 01729 0206
01729 0231

THUNDER BALLOONS U.S.A.
BOX 9
LOOKOUT MOUNTAIN
TENNESSEE 37350
U.S.A.

PHONE 404-820-1641

SEE
ROCK
CITY

If you have enjoyed BALLOONING: A PICTORIAL GUIDE & WORLD DIRECTORY, you may wish to become a member of the Balloon Federation of America. All members receive Ballooning, a colorful and most interesting magazine and in addition, licensed pilot members also receive the Pilot Newsletter. (There is no relationship between this directory and the BFA.) For details you may contact:

The Balloon Federation of America
A Division of the National Aeronautic Association
Suite 610, 806 15th Street N.W.,
Washington, D.C. 20005

The author is a member of the BFA and would be pleased to have this publication mentioned in your correspondence.

KEEP LOOKING UP

HEBREWS 13:8 "JESUS CHRIST THE SAME YES-
TERDAY, AND
TODAY AND FOREVER"